"Just when you think you have these fish figured out they prove you stupid."

Captain Brad Durick

Noel,
Always great fun cattin w/ the
Coors. See you next time,

CRACKING THE CHANNEL CATFISH CODE

Brad Durick

Redcats Media and Promotions LLC
1640 King Cove
Grand Forks, ND 58201
www.redcatsmedia.com
701-739-5808

ISBN-13: 978-0615849942
ISBN-10: 0615849946

Table of Contents

Forward

Welcome to Cracking the Channel Catfish Code.

13 years ago, Brad Durick knew little about catfish let alone how to catch them.

Once that first Red River of the North pig hit, he was hooked as they say.

What typically is a casual summer pastime for most catfish anglers became an obsession for Captain Brad.

Don't scoff at the captain title, either. It's official. He earned it through a rigorous U.S. Coast Guard program. He's a licensed fishing guide. He spends more time on the water zeroing in on catching trophy cats than any angler I know. High water doesn't stop him either. He's been known to run the Red River dam north of Grand Forks, N.D., when 12 feet of water racing across its top.

Durick sees rivers how you and I watch a sci-fi movie while wearing those damnable 3D goggles: shallow, deep, current, eddy, sides – even in the trees (flooded, of course). His ability to visualize how fish are reacting to their environment takes practice by spending an average of 75 days on the water from spring through September.

Truly, Durick's appetite for the river, the fish and, together, the incredible resource that is the mighty Red, is exceeded only by the hunger of a pre-spawn female catfish.

This is good -- good because he's sharing what he's learned with readers, not just in this book, though. National media outlets, such as In-Fisherman and Midwest Outdoors, have taken notice. He's guided the guys who write and shoot the videos on bunches of trips, always with one goal in mind: catch trophy catfish (and release them). Did I mention he guides?

In these pages, you will learn about how the book took root. Brad will discuss a bit about key catfish gear; how to anchor (you bet it matters); tales about the barometer and how it may or may not affect fishing; water temperature, metabolism and more. The information on electronics, particularly side imaging, will blow your mind, make you think.

But, the most important information in the book, the most useful stuff if you're really interested in the nerdy side of catfishing, can be found in Chapter 4 : "River Flow." There you will explore concepts such as "optimum flow range," "secondary current," and how fish relate to their ever changing environment. The Red River carves its way north toward Lake Winnipeg, which is unusual enough for a North American River. But it also flows through some of the flattest and most fertile ag land in the country. The river is brown because it's silty. It looks tame but it isn't. The river's northern current during high flow can rip 100-foot tall trees out by their roots in a heartbeat. The Red's flooding of both land and cities is legendary and tragic.

Cracking the Channel Catfish Code is no fish tale. It's packed with useful information. These tools, tips and techniques apply to any river or tributary in the country. So enjoy the read. We hope you learn a thing or two. And if you know something Brad doesn't, drop him a line at redrivercatfish.com.

Kevin Grinde, who was willingly reeled in to edit this book.

Acknowledgements

My wife **Lisa Durick** for dealing with my constant talking about and working on this project and her proofreading skills.

Kevin Grinde for his editing and advice.

Brad Dokken for the cover photo and just being a friend through this process.

Doug Stange from In-Fisherman Magazine and TV for allowing me to visit with him on the origins of his catfish expertise.

Keith Sutton, author of many catfishing books for his time to discuss who the 21st Century catfish anglers is.

Jake Bussolini, author of The Catfish Hunters for opening my mind that barometer may not be the key to bad days on the water.

Lynn Schueter for all his expertise in fish biology, his patience to answer questions and spur more thought to prove the theories in this book.

Margaret Laumb for making my terrible drawings look good.

Steve Kelsch from the University of North Dakota Biology Department for allowing me the time to discuss their catfish research and how they conducted it.

Cory Schmidt for his expertise in 21st century electronics.

Tyler George for sharing his expertise on ice fishing channel catfish.

Brian Klawitter discussing his video findings on how catfish react under ice.

Rob Neumann from In-Fisherman Magazine and TV for discussing my findings and showing interest in the new information provided.

David Ashby, owner of Bottom Dwellers Tackle, for his time discussing new catfishing rods and products.

Doug Rice, catfish angler for giving me an insight into another part of the country and what he looks for in new gear and boats.

Iowa Sportsman Magazine for support and allowing me to use a graphic.

Cat River Anchors for loving the catfishing world and building the best anchor on the market.

CHAPTER 1:
WELCOME ABOARD

Catfishing could be one of the most misunderstood angling pastimes in the fishing community.

The widespread perception that catfish anglers are just a bunch of muddy, old hicks doesn't help. But the truth these days is a long cast away from that old school yarn. In fact, over the past decade, catfishing's popularity has grown in leaps and runs across the United States – especially in the North, according to tournament participation and fisheries surveys.

Until recently, other popular fish species, such as bass and walleyes, have received the bulk of scientific research dollars and time by both biologists and anglers who seek how environmental factors affect fish. There's digital libraries out there filled with information – much of it technical -- about how to find and catch more bass and 'eyes and crappies and trout.

As for catfish, the information is tougher to find. Every catfisherman, especially old timers, have their own theories about how each external factor affects channel cats. Some say cats bite the best when the barometer is low; others just the opposite; and still others say they prefer to fish just before the barometer starts its plunge.

And what about the moon? Some cat guys say the fish bite the best with no moon, while some say they bite the best with a full moon. Many catfish anglers simply say the day was good or bad and all of the other factors are just over thinking the simplicity and relaxation of what catfishing offers.

This book is different from other published information about catfishing because it probes in-depth the world of river channel catfish. It attempts to crack the code about the external environmental factors that affect fish behavior. And most importantly, it teaches you how to catch more trophy catfish.

The book also delves into the social aspects of catfishing and reveals some stories of both success and failure. This book is not a "how-to" beginner's guide to catching channel cats. This book starts where all others end. The goal here is to make you a better channel catfish angler through greater knowledge of catfish and the rivers where they live.

In this book I will explain who the 21st Century catfish anglers are and how they affect the future of the sport.

I will explain:

- How environmental factors affect river channel cats and offer some solutions on how to stay on fish. These factors are river flow, barometer, water temperature, and catfish metabolism.
- How moon phases and solunar times affect channel catfish.
- How the new concept of lateral movement affects fish habits.
- How catfish behave in the various seasons ranging from spring's cold water through the summer spawn, and finally into fall. Each season contains specific patterning to help you predict the bite and catch more channel cats.

Towards the end I will explore 21st century electronics and explain how to use them.

The book will also show you some indicators that will help you put this new knowledge to work for you in your river. These are tried and true theories that have been tested both on paper and on the water. Enjoy the book and good fishing to you in the future.

CATFISH TIP- Simply keeping small notes of what is and isn't working on a given day can be used as a teaching tool for the future.

PROJECT BACKGROUND

In 2010, the Red River of the North on the Minnesota/North Dakota border found itself in yet another wet year that began with a hard winter and evolved into an extended spring flood. Land along the river was so saturated that every time it rained two inches or more the runoff caused the river to rise three to five feet. The high water events of 2010 would last anywhere from five days to two weeks depending on which part of the drainage received the runoff.

From a fishing guide's perspective, it was like fishing on a bouncing ball. Nobody was having much luck with the catfish. Knowing I could not shut down for every flood, I had to find a way to catch fish in these ever changing conditions.

First, I went back to my old standby for catfish information: "Catfish Fever" (the best catfish how-to book ever published in my opinion) written by In-Fisherman's Doug Stange, Steve Quinn, and Otis "Toad" Smith. As I re-read the book I could not find anything that specifically answered my questions about fishing when water levels fluctuated.

I headed to the and trolled for information. I scoured the Web for days and found nothing. It was almost as if nobody had ever looked into the fluctuating water conditions phenomena let alone how to combat it to catch fish. The questions remained: Do anglers just quit fishing because of the high water or is the issue simply few fishermen understand how to catch fish in these conditions? As it turns out, the answer is a blend of both -- but nobody I could find had ever really investigated the topic and written about it.

Still fishing for info, I took a chance and wrote Doug Stange from In-Fisherman a letter asking if he had any answers on the subject. Stange is an authority on catfishing. I look up to the guy who wrote the best book on the subject. He had to have answers, I figured. He wrote back to me explaining that he had never really looked into fishing high water that deep and 2010 was a weird, wet year for everyone. I thanked him for writing and told him I would keep fishing and looking for answers.

So I began my journey to figure out how to catch in the tough times. I started with a few simple questions:

- Why does fishing get poor when the high water events happen?
- Where do the fish go?
- How do I catch them?

I began my research for this book in 2010. In the years since, I have spoken with many experienced catfish anglers and a few old timers. When questioning them about these topics, I found that many know how to make the adjustments to stay on fish. But when I dug deeper as to why and how they changed their fishing approach, they said they "just do" and had no concrete answer beyond that.

One of the questions I asked the old timers was, "When the water is constantly fluctuating, what do you do?" Some said they stayed home and others said they just kept fishing until the fish turned back on.

Another question I asked was, "When the water gets high what kind of adjustments do you make?" The answer from the hardcore guys was: "Go shallow." When pressed, anglers said they wanted to avoid debris or, simply because that's where the new shoreline moved. Lastly, I asked about barometer movement and how anglers reacted to location and presentation. The answers varied widely and there was no real conclusion to be drawn. As you can see, many of these questions had few or no concrete answers. That's because everybody has different approaches to fishing -- and most don't have to make a living fishing in all conditions.

My research continued. I started visiting the United States Geological Survey (USGS) Web site to find the historical data for the 2010 season. I correlated that info on the printouts with catch rates I kept from each day on the water. On the charts I could clearly see the ups and downs of the river levels as clearly as I could see my catch rates. For the most part the lines were practically married to each other. That led me to believe that the fish were still biting -- but where and how? Luckily, I had catch rates and pattern notes for the previous three seasons, too. Now I had to go back to see if other years contained the trends I was seeing from my current year.

I then began to blend what I learned on the computer to what I was experiencing on the water. One day I noticed a funny looking current seam identified by the fallen seeds from cottonwood trees that line the river banks. The white fuzz was moving at about half the speed of the current in the main river channel. I tried fishing this current seam and, to my amazement, caught a ton of fish. And what do you know – I discovered a pattern and that day my "Secondary Current Theory" was born. Later in this book, in Chapter 4, on river flow, we will explore this in greater detail.

I soon realized that I'd answered one question, but the old adage of the more you learn the less you know began to surface like a school of feeding goldeyes. I soon found myself wondering about cold fronts, moon phase and seasonal transitions.

I remembered some of my disastrous days I'd had on the water following cold fronts. I consulted my data and realized I needed more information. I started looking up other factors that could pertain to catfishing to see how they fit into the puzzle. I knew if I understood how the fish were reacting in certain unusual environmental conditions, I could make adjustments to locations and presentations to continue catching fish, even during the tough times.

I assembled the data and ran graphs to evaluate how the factors affected catfishing, I started to notice one other factor was playing a huge part in catfishing success: the barometer. I was noticing that if the barometer was stable or slowly rising or falling there was virtually no change in fishing success. In fact, more often than not, success increased. But if the barometer took a steep plunge I would have a disastrous day or series of days on the water. This phenomenon showed up repeatedly over the years. I really thought I was onto something with the barometer, but still did not have concrete patterns to put fish in the net during the tough times that were created by the cold fronts. In Chapter 6, on barometer, you will see that I was on the right track with my theories about barometric pressure. I learned ultimately that the real key to successful channel catfishing was reading and interpreting water temperature.

I needed another season of working out the concepts of secondary current and barometer to realize that my theories were only partly on target. I was quickly able to figure out the answer to the original question of how fish behave when the river rises and falls. I still did not have the answers about behavior in connection to barometric pressure.

My work continued on the water. I needed nearly an entire season to realize how water temperature corresponds to catfish metabolism and, hence, how to pattern the fish accordingly based on food requirements. Through hours and hours on the water, I learned the most important part of patterning channel catfish throughout the season is water temperature.

You now know about my project, how it all started and where it has led. Of course answering the rest of these questions has led to even more questions that need more research and thought. For now, I believe that understanding various environmental concepts -- flow, barometer, water temperature, and metabolism – can help an angler determine how they affect catfish and, in turn, help you catch more fish – especially trophy catfish.

MY RESEARCH GOALS

If you can answer how environmental factors affect channel catfish on a river and how these factors relate to feeding and seasonal movement, catfish behavior will become easier to predict allowing you to make location adjustments, and how to adjust lure or bait size to catch more fish.

By the end of this book you should be able to see how the following factors play into channel catfish activity.

External Factors of River Channel Catfish

- ➢ River Level
- ➢ River Flow
- ➢ Barometric Pressure
- ➢ Water Temperature
- ➢ Metabolism
- ➢ Moon Phase

River Level: River depth is based on how deep the water is at a given gauge. It may also be reported in elevation above sea level. (Also referred to as river height.)

River Flow: The amount of water transferred through the channel at any given time. It is measured in cubic feet per second.

Water Temperature: The actual temperature of the water as measured by the data collection site. It may be reported in Celsius or Fahrenheit.

Barometric Pressure: The force per unit area exerted against a surface by the weight of air above that surface in the Earth's atmosphere.

Moon Phase: The appearance of the illuminated portion of the Moon as seen by an observer. The lunar phases vary cyclically as the Moon orbits the Earth, according to the changing relative positions of the Earth, Moon and Sun.

Catch Rate: Measured in fish per hour (number of fish caught divided by hours fished).

Metabolism: The set of chemical reactions that happen in the cells of living organisms to sustain life. These processes allow organisms to grow and reproduce, maintain their structures, and respond to their environment. The word metabolism can also refer to all chemical reactions that occur in living organisms, including digestion and the transport of substances into and between different cells.

Lateral Movement: Moving perpendicular from the middle to the outside edge of the river rather than parallel up and down stream.

RESEARCH SOURCES

I am basing all of the research and findings in this book on data that I have personally collected. The research used for this book was collected and interpreted to improve my catch rates. I have no formal education or background in biology. All data in this book have been collected from respected organizations as well as my own on-the-water observations and record keeping. L. R. Schlueter, retired fisheries biologist, North Dakota Game and Fish and American Fisheries Society *Certified Fisheries Scientist* who specialized in catfish on the Red River for many years, advised me on the accuracy of the research and assisted in answering other questions about fish biology. He also assisted in data collection and analysis to maintain scientific integrity.

Flow Data

In this book, you will read much about "flow" and phrases such as "optimum flow range." Flow research was the original inspiration for this entire project. The collection of flow data comes from one source, the United States Geological Survey (USGS), which keeps historical records dating back more than 100 years. It also keeps real time data for all gauges that can be accessed via the at any time.

Current flow data can be called up to create a custom report which is then distributed in the form of a graph. Some of the graph numbers are hard to interpret for data entry and have been rounded to the nearest quarter foot for the ease of use. While this may be off by a fraction in some cases, it supplies the basis for all trending that is then matched to the catch notes and pattern notes of this research.

Most USGS flow data used in this project were taken from the East Grand Forks, Minnesota, and the Drayton, North Dakota, gauges. It should also be noted that both of the Grand Forks areas and the Drayton area have boat accesses that are above and below dams. Both gauges are located above the respected dams. Although most of the fishing used in this book was done on the downstream side of the dams, some was done above. This fact does alter some actual flow data in reality simply because dams obviously slow down water. But because flow data was used throughout my research, it is consistent and accurate as can be.

Barometer Data

I found that knowing barometric pressure is very critical to the patterning of channel catfish in rivers. Fish activity may not be due to direct effects of the barometer but the predictors it offers I found valuable.

To collect barometric data, historical information was collected based on the zip code of 58201, which is Grand Forks, North Dakota. It was obtained from the "History Data" application from www.wunderground.com. Weather Underground keeps weather data far beyond barometer such as air temperature, wind speed and direction, and precipitation.

Having this data available allows for other aspects of weather to be used as needed for future research. This data is the most accurate place to locate the barometric pressure data need and can also be reviewed for other factors that may be needed to answer further questions.

Temperature Data

Similar to the flow data used in this research, the water temperature data was collected as historical data from the USGS. Readings were taken at the East Grand Forks, Minnesota, gauge for the entire river system. The USGS has kept on file temperature records dating back to 2007. For this reason, none of the temperature data in relation to catch records were used before 2007.

Some of the flow data was taken from Drayton, North Dakota, gauge even though it does not record temperature data. The Drayton area is approximately 60 river miles downstream from East Grand Forks. I used temperature data at the East Grand Forks, Minnesota gauge.

Metabolism Data

Unlike USGS data for water flow and water temperature there is no magic web site to collect historical data. All metabolism data had to be developed based on a numbering system provided in a fish metabolism chart. This chart was provided by L.R. Schlueter. The basis used for the metabolism research was a numerical system that was determinant on the water temperature to indicate the increased or decreased metabolism.

This information has been confirmed by similar data found on the that correspond fairly close to the original one provided by L.R. Schlueter. Based on the research, the original charts seemed to be accurate enough to accomplish the goals of this research.

To prove the metabolism numbers were accurate, they were cross-checked with channel catfish farming studies based on metabolism rates for maximum growth and how channel catfish on farms in closed systems rely on water temperature to maintain or gain maximum weight. Then food requirements were transformed from fish in captivity to what wild fish need to survive.

The chart and catfish farming studies match almost identical showing that the channel catfish temperature requirements in the wild along the same levels as they would to gain maximum weight in an aquacultural environment. It is also expected that a catfish living in the wild would require more food to make up for the extra energy spent on the survival of living in current and hunting for food.

Moon Phase Data

Moon phase data are available online from many sources. They are printed in most fishing and outdoor magazines and can be accessed easily at any time. For this project, past data was collected from www.moonphases.info. From the data collection to the graphing format a numbering system was developed where the full moon was given a value of 15 and a new moon was given a value of zero. On the graph, the numbers increase from zero to 15 then back down to zero. This numbering system allowed for easy analysis and graphing of how the moon affected catch rates.

Catch Notes

Catch notes are the most important part of this research project. They are the core that unites all other information and make this entire project come together. With each day of fishing, I made a record of how many fish were landed, how many hours were fished and any other highlights of the outing. Patterns were noted as to what worked and what didn't. Here's what it looks like:

Date	River Flow	Water Temp	Fish/Hour	Barometer	Metabolism	Moon
10-May-12	4.9	15.5	2	29.7	4.25	10
11-May-12	4.8	16	1.5	30.04	4.5	9
12-May-12	4.8	16.5	1.8	30.21	4.75	8
13-May-12	4.6	17	1.5	29.99	5	7
14-May-12	4.6	17	2.25	29.85	5	6
15-May-12	4.6	18		30.06	6	5
16-May-12	4.6	18	1.38	30.03	6	4
17-May-12	4.6	18		29.59	6	3
18-May-12	4.3	18.5	1.25	29.55	6.5	2
19-May-12	4.2	19		29.77	7	1
20-May-12	4.1	18.5	1.5	30.1	6.5	0
21-May-12	4	18.25	1.6	30.06	6	1

> The chart above is an example of data kept in Microsoft Excel for referral and to build the graphs used in this book.

Here are the results of good record keeping and putting the research system together over time to produce success: Two lunker fall channel catfish!

It should be noted that I began keeping records in 2007. This project did not begin until 2010. The records for the first three years were very vague with only hours fished and number of fish caught being recorded. With the help of the , I filled in many of the blanks by going back and finding the missing environmental data. The years ranging from 2010 through 2012 had much more accurate pattern notes; I knew which questions to ask and what to look for and keep track of.

To cross check my pattern notes, in 2011, Captain Kent Hollands, another licensed Coast Guard captain and licensed Red River catfish guide, also kept a season's worth of pattern notes and catch records for this project. At the end of the season we compared catch notes and other notes about patterns that were both successful and unsuccessful. Much of what we found matched. I believe that helps prove that most of the catch records were accurate. While Captain Hollands only participated in the study one season that information helped to allow me to understand future patterns during high water situations.

WORK IN PROGRESS

This research project is a work in progress and I've got plenty of patterns that have not been perfected. Time and research have led me this far allowing me to write this book. I believe I've cracked what I call the Catfish Code.

In the early years of the research I was fishing spots, not patterns, that were relative to the information I had. What that means is I was fishing the same "spot" in the river no matter what the conditions were. Over time I developed patterns to match conditions using groups of spots. When I review the catch notes of the early years and see the declines in catch rates, it's simple for me to see now that the causes of many poor days were a direct outcome of fishing the wrong pattern.

Catch notes are the key to this project and to teaching you how to be a more effective catfish angler in rivers – or in any body of water for that matter. Even as this book is going to print there is ongoing research to tighten the patterns for continued success. Hopefully, as you read on, you can crack the catfish code in your river too.

CHAPTER 2:

THE SOCIETY OF CATFISHING IN THE 21st CENTURY

Catfish anglers are an interesting bunch.

Sort of secretive yet they're as good as any angler you will find in the United States.

Catfish remain the fourth most sought after fish in the United States, according to the US Fish and Wildlife Service. This is a statistic that dates back to at least the 1970s. The popularity of catfishing is behind only that of bass and panfish (including crappies) and is neck and neck with trout.

Back in the 1970s and 1980s, when the first catfish articles and books were being published, the average catfish angler was into the simple enjoyment of catching catfish and feeding their families. They were viewed by the "elite" species anglers as some sort of a "second class" angler. The gear and methods of catching the catfish were simple and inexpensive yet effective.

Where has catfishing evolved since the beginning of the 21st century?

All of my catfishing is in the new century. Beginning in 2000, when I tied into my first catfish, an obsession was born. Of course, like many hooked anglers, I bought the books and read anything I could get my hands on. I worked hard to learn the fishing basics and understanding electronics was a huge part of the learning process. I used the depth finder to look for holes and break lines where catfish lurked. I also used electronics to learn the lay of the land but never really understood what I was looking at.

Even after becoming a catfish guide I kept trying to learn the secrets of the fish. I used electronics first and basic river and catfish knowledge second. I upgraded and used the newest and best equipment including side imaging sonar with the goal of utilizing the modern marvels to learn the river. The technology allowed me to put my fishing on the forefront of catching channel catfish in the new decade.

While I was learning how to catch catfish through research, sweat and modern technology, I was just one person in a new movement of catfish anglers who also were also moving into the 21st century. These like-minded catfish fanatics were learning all they could and attempting to catch more and larger fish. Anglers were learning the techniques and making contacts to learn more as the catfish world took to the .

The age has helped arm a new generation of catfish anglers with new ideas on how to utilize technology and fuel a new desire to target and land trophy catfish in particular. Over the past decade, it seemed for many in the catfishing industry that there was a great increase in catfish anglers. Reality suggests this may not be the case. For sure, though, this new generation of catfish anglers entering the public eye was giving the world of catfishing a new face.

I interviewed outdoor writer and catfishing expert Keith Sutton for his view on the evolution of catfishing and the catfish angler. "It is not that catfishing has gotten any more popular, it is just that it has gotten more attention than in the past giving it a new look," he said.

 Doug Stange, the veteran catfish writer from In-Fisherman Magazine and TV, agrees with Sutton's statement. Stange said he agrees that with the new found ability to catch trophy catfish, the sport is becoming more important not only to the catfish community but the fishing community as a whole. Both men agreed that the number of catfish anglers is about the same as it was 30 years ago. But angler goals have changed from feeding the family to catching trophies. Ethics have changed, too. Catfish conservation is important to most of this new generation of catfish angler. They are more interested in the experience of photographing and releasing fish for the next person to catch rather than killing the finite resource, especially with trophy cats.

So who is a 21st century catfish angler? The fishermen who just want to sit by the river for a leisurely day and maybe catch enough fish to eat are still there. Their skills and knowledge has been passed down through the generations and still very effective. And there are the weekend warriors who want to catch some fish for the table and maybe a trophy to boot.

The new class of catfish anglers are the rod and reel only group who have shied away or even shunned the use of other catfishing methods, such as trotlines, limb lines, or jug lines. This new class has one thing on their minds when they fish: trophy fish and the fight that ensues when they tie into them.

This group tends to be hard core. They enjoy learning everything they can about the fish, the gear and the electronics. They want to put the whole puzzle together to find, catch and conquer trophy catfish. This is the same group of anglers that are very passionate about selective harvest and promoting catch and release of all trophy catfish. It is this group of anglers that mostly make up the World Wide Web community and buys the magazines and books to learn as much about catfish as they can whenever they can.

In 1989, when Doug Stange and the In-Fisherman staff wrote "Catfish Fever," they mentioned that there really was not a "professional" catfish angler. That's changed. Now there is one other demographic that is more of an extension of the modern trophy catfish angler than a separate group: the tournament angler. Human nature dictates there is always a desire to compete for fun (and for money). Like bass or walleye tournaments, the past decade has seen many new tournaments spring up all over the country allowing these anglers to compete, sometimes on the national stage. Indeed, the 21st century has brought forth the era of the professional catfish angler. There are now many catfish pros around the country attempting to eke out a living catching fish. There also are many truly professional catfish guides, tournament pros, and promoters.

But the level of sophistication catfish anglers employ now wouldn't have taken place without Stange and In-Fisherman writing and filming catfishing stories, books, and TV as far back as the late 1970s. Stange said that was an exciting time in the world of catfishing because the sport lacked the knowledge, skill and finesse necessary to crack the catfish code and thereby putting more and bigger fish in the boat. Stange was a pioneer in teaching the basic theories that many of the catfish anglers use 20 plus years later whether the anglers know it or not.

Expert Keith Sutton says there is no other species of fish in the United States that offers a person the chance of catching a state or world record specimen. This new generation loves big fish and the media has caught on; it pays attention because they know that everyone loves to see big fish.

What all of this means is that catfishing, thanks to the experts who paved the way 20 years ago, now competes with some of the more traditionally visible species such as bass and walleyes. The technology age has moved the sport forward because more information is available to more people and the stigma of catching catfish has been replaced with the desire to catch big fish. The new catfish angler is eager to learn and pursue the sport to the highest level.

A CHAT WITH IN-FISHERMAN'S DOUG STANGE

While researching this book the opportunity to interview a true pioneer of modern catfishing, Doug Stange, Managing Editor of In-Fisherman Magazine and Television, arose. The reason for this interview was not necessarily to learn more about catching channel cats but to talk to the man who has written about and promoted catfishing for more than 30 years. The goal was to hear from the source where catfishing has been and where it will go.

Stange, a teacher at the time, first started writing about catfishing in the 1970s because catfishing was his passion and nobody was telling the story about the species at that time. He eventually got a job with In-Fisherman Magazine where he made catfishing articles an important part of the publication that still stands today.

"Catfish Fever" changed catfishing forever. It was the first and still best book of its kind. It teaches the basics every angler should know about understanding and catching catfish. It covers everything from bait selection to gear selection then teaches us all how to better catch a catfish.

The run-riffle-hole theory that was introduced and written about at length in "Catfish Fever" is the basis for any channel catfishing in rivers. It is this theory that most modern channel catfishing is tailored after. During the interview, Stange told the story of how he figured out the run-riffle-hole theory that he ultimately based a big part of his career on.

He said in his younger days he noticed in a small river with very clear water how the water would run flat then riffle up and eventually flatten back out into the hole. He said he could stand on the bank and see what the water was doing and right where the water was flowing into the hole he could see fish. He noted the fish were using the head of the hole off the riffle for feeding and using the deeper parts of the hole and the other cover to rest, digest and recover.

The run-riffle-hole theory was what led Stange to the many stories about catfish. It remains a proud moment for him and he knows that he laid the groundwork for much of what has come about in the past 20 plus years.

"Catfisherman have always known they are important to the world of fishing, but now they have become an important part of the fishing world in the eyes of others." He knows that catfish anglers have always been an integral part of the catfishing world but nobody ever told their story until he did.

So where is catfishing heading? Stange cannot say. What he does know is that he set the table for catfishing and now, with advancements in technology and anglers' desire to learn more and improve on catching more and bigger fish, the sport still has a long way to go.

CHAPTER 3:

GEAR FOR THE 21ST CENTURY

Multispecies anglers have their own arsenals of gear, depending on which fish they happen to be targeting. The muskie maniacs are known for their plugs and spinner baits; the bass guys like their worms; the walleye group, their jigs. The 21st century catfish angler is no different. The problem is catfishing gear has lagged in the advances other tackle has made. The good news is that the changes in catfishing tackle, boats and electronics are quickly evolving into more sophisticated choices all designed to do one thing: catch more and larger catfish.

Catfish Rods

In my own catfishing, gear has changed a lot the last few years. How I use this equipment to be more effective has also changed. Over the years of buying and testing rods (and there are many to choose from) I have settled on a custom rod by Blackhorse Custom Rods based in Missouri. I made the switch to customs mainly because they are crafted with higher quality eyelets -- and I get to pick the blanks that are used to give me a uniform fight in every rod.

The reason I like a custom rod is I know I will be able to have the control of a catfish and not have to worry about weak points in the rod that may cause it to break in the heat of battle. Also, having more eyelets that are placed closer together on a balanced blank will allow the line to run straighter and not twist off the rod with a big fish. These small things can mean a lot when you fish as much as I do or you have the fish of a lifetime on the line.

There are still many catfish anglers around the country who are using the cheaper end of the mass produced rods and this is fine. There are many great high quality production rods on the market. With the increased popularity of trophy fishing for the biggest catfish, however, there is a growing demographic of catfish anglers that demand more than the one-size-fits-all rod. They want a variety of rods that are manufactured to match a specific application and need.

Since about 2008, there has been a resurgence of the catfish specific rod and this time they are here to stay. There are now numerous rods built to outfit every angler's needs, especially for blue cats. The channel cat specific rod is still lagging behind blue cat equipment somewhat, but they are evolving and will soon be on the market.

According to David Ashby, owner of Bottom Dwellers Tackle, the trend aimed at rod improvement is happening nationwide. Ashby says that since he opened his store in 2009 he has seen a dramatic shift from the cheaper rods to a higher quality "catfish specific" rod. These rods have been designed to handle the rigors of fishing large fish. He says the shift from the cheaper rods has changed to a ratio of "20:1 in favor of higher end rods. The biggest reason serious catfish anglers are now buying higher end gear is because time is limited and they don't want to lose the fish of a lifetime due to poor quality gear."

Fifteen years ago there was some dabbling in the higher end, catfish specific rod but the development was greeted with little fanfare from customers. Those rods are now extinct but those anglers who still use them enjoy them and make up an almost cult following. These fans are willing to pay hundreds of dollars to acquire their favorite discontinued rod off the .

According to Illinois catfish angler Doug Rice, who is a long-time fan of those rods, said that they have a very loyal fan base who are willing to pay to find one of the old originals. Rice went on to say that the original Berkley E-Cat and the St. Croix Classic Catfish rod had a price point that in the day was just too expensive for most who wanted a top notch catfish rod. Today if those rods were marketed would have a more palatable price. The failure of those rods is proof that the market dictates which products live and die. At the time, they died because of a lack of willingness among those in the catfish to pay the price and support such an advanced catfish rod.

Ashby from Bottom Dwellers Tackle agreed, saying the rods were great rods but were "simply ahead of their time."

At the same time rods have advanced greatly, catfishing reels have really not changed all that much. In the 1989 In-Fisherman book, "Catfish Fever," one of the reels most mentioned was the 6500 c3 baitcaster by Abu Garcia. The 6500 c3 and other similar baitcast models remain basically unchanged other than some superficial modifications. Of course there have been new reels released that are said to be better but, all in all, good catfishing reels tend to remain the same as they have been for decades.

Hooks and Terminal Tackle

Hooks are another area where the catfish angler has plowed ahead and demanded superior quality gear over the past few years. The advances in fishing hooks for cats have helped allow the trophy angler to mature by leaps and bounds. The biggest change is a hook that was adapted from salt water fishing to become a mainstay in 21st century catfishing. This is the circle hook. The circle hook is nothing new in the grand scheme of fishing, but with the desire to release most trophy fish, the circle hook has found its place in most tackle boxes.

The circle hook has a curved beak that must be fished a bit differently than a normal fish hook. This hook must be "loaded up" on the rod to gain proper hook penetration. When the fish takes the bait, the hook will turn into the corner of its mouth allowing for a nearly perfect hook set 99 percent of the time. This perfect hooking in the corner of the mouth makes for quick non-injuring removal and allows for a safe release of the fish.

Bottom Dwellers Tackle owner, David Ashby, said that high quality hooks are another area where the catfish angler has really stepped up. Back in the day, a cheap hook was all you needed. Now a quality hook is as important to the big picture as using a quality rod and reel to ensure the successful landing of a trophy fish.

With rods and hooks making big leaps forward, what about other tackle? And just how has the catfish tackle industry changed? According to an article in the April 2013 issue of Fishing Tackle Retailer magazine, the catfish tackle industry has been largely ignored. It went on to say that stocking an array of hooks and other quality catfishing gear to satisfy the catfish enthusiast can prove to be a profit center for any shop. Stock them and they will be bought.

Catfishing Boats

Another demand from the catfishing community over the past decade is in catfishing boats. It did not take me long in my guiding career to want something that was more useful than a V hull and better to work in, plus keep clients safe and comfortable. In my situation, it was a G3 Gator Tough Jon Boat. What drew me to a big jon boat was the stability, ease of movement within, and the center console for increased driving visibility.

Most jons such as my G3 are wide and flat bottom, which allows me the ability to move quickly and keep my customers comfortable all day. The G3 is also very easy to clean and set up from day to day. In comparison to some of the more popular V bottom boats that are set up more for storage and trolling techniques, it comes down to space and ability to set lines and fight fish comfortably. Each situation has a different requirement, but for the most part, a large jon boat can be the perfect catfish boat for my needs.

While my needs were for a good wide catfish boat, the 21st century catfisherman (especially where blue cats are king) demanded even more in a good catfish boat.

Professional catfish angler, Doug Rice: "Things have changed" since the early part of the 2000s in the boat world. As the needs of catfishermen changed, so have the boats. "Tournament anglers want boats that can be customized to their needs with huge livewells to carry huge catfish to weigh in."

Right now Sea Ark now holds a comfortable lead in the catfish boat market. Companies such as G3 already make great catfishing boats, but none quite as tournament specific.

Electronics

After talking about big customized catfishing boats, it would be a crime not to mention high end electronics. Electronics have come a long way in catfishing over the past five to seven years. Even in my own guide service, I now use the high end Humminbird side sonar with GPS on a daily basis. Catman Cory Schmidt from Traditions Media, who represents Humminbird, had to admit that this new technology was not developed with the catfish angler in mind but it has crept into the sport in a big way. Side imaging has taken over the catfishing world, especially in the tournament angling and in the blue catfish pastime.

While controlled drifting and trolling for cats is not part of the material in this book, I should mention that one other area where electronics are taking over the catfish world is the combination of Minn Kota I Pilot and Humminbird that creates the I-Pilot Link. According to Schmidt, this technology allows total control over the area of trolling or controlled drifting and it is all tied together by the depth finder and the trolling motor making the presentation more effective than it has ever been.

Another new release by Humminbird that may prove very useful to the catfish angler is 360 Imaging. This is a unit that works with the HD units to allow the angler to see sonar at any angle within 360 degrees of the boat. As of this writing, the 360 is just being released so only time will tell if it proves to be as useful to anglers as it seems it could be.

In many cases, the catfish angler still uses fairly simple gear, but the new generation of catfisherman is starting to demand more in an attempt to catch more fish and have the best technology and comforts available.

Like the bass and walleye business, the catfishing industry will continue to grow and evolve. This progression will ultimately grow an industry while making catfish anglers more effective at catching the mighty catfish in the 21st century.

CHAPTER 4:

RIVER FLOW

Understanding river flow is one of the most important aspects of catching channel catfish.

If you understand rivers and how flow changes the makeup of the river -- and how channel cats react -- you are ahead of most anglers.

At the beginning of this book, I explained that one year I saw the river fluctuate two to five feet with every rain event. It was during that roller coaster season that the research that led to this book came to life. It was at that point when I realized that nearly everything a catfish does in terms of movement and location can be understood by learning how current works.

There are two ways to measure rivers: flow and gauge readings. Most people choose to use river level readings (gauge height) before they examine river flow because gauge height is measured in feet of water, which is a term that most people understand for their local river. This is fine because many of the gauges provided by United States Geological Survey (USGS) only provide gauge height to measure levels.

River level and flow directly correspond with each other, though, so you can use them interchangeably when measuring your specific river. From here on in this book we will be using flow as the more useful definition. That's because measuring flow in cubic feet per second (CFS) is universal to all rivers while gauge height is not.

When I first started keeping records on flow, I noticed that I was always catching more catfish when the river was within a particular "flow range." This "flow range" forms when the river rises or falls within a certain window of cubic feet per second. This epiphany led me to start looking into what is now called "optimum flow range." During that wet summer, I was still fishing the same spots and using the same techniques no matter what the flow was doing. As I fished more and research continued, I found that making slight adjustments according to flow triggered an increase in catch rates.

OPTIMUM FLOW RANGE

Every river has an optimum flow range when there is a window in the river flow. For fish, that means catfish will feed aggressively along current breaks, current spots, tailraces and holes. If you can establish this range in your river, you can almost guarantee catching more and bigger fish.

Fishing is almost always good when a river is in optimum flow. This window may be over a very short time period in some smaller rivers and very spread out in larger rivers. On the Red River of the North, for example, the window of flow range is only about 3500 CFS. When the flow rises above or falls below the optimum flow range, the fish will change patterns and we must go to work to find them.

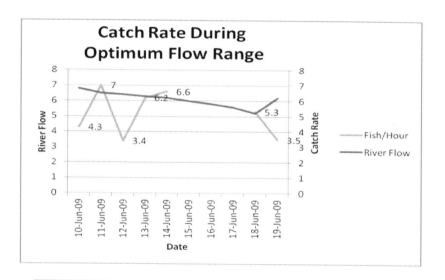

The graph above shows that the river flow was stable but dropped slightly during an eight-day period. Of course you can see the catch rates rise and fall and vary about three fish per hour from day to day. This variation in catch rate has more to do with move times (staying on a spot too long) and angler experience than what the graph trends.

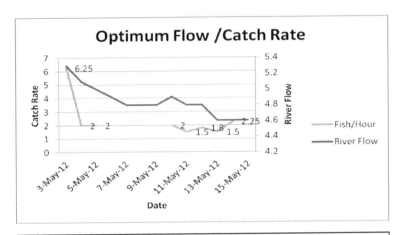

This chart shows the flows as they drop into the flow rate and right back out of the flow rate on the low end. You can see that as the flow was entering optimum flow range, fishing was out of this world. Then the flow and the bite leveled off into a very consistent pattern. The fish spread out in the river after the flow went below optimum.

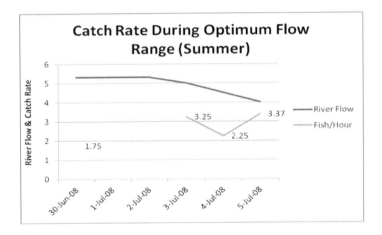

This chart shows a great example of optimum flow range in respect to the catfish bite. The flow was higher than average during post-spawn at this time in July. Normal baseline catch rates are around 1.5 fish per hour. When the river is within flow range, the fish are actively feeding and the catch rates rise 100 to 110 percent when fished aggressively during the optimum flow range.

Over the years, I have found a location that will only produce channel catfish consistently when the river is within optimum flow range. In just this few hundred yards of river, many stories of great fishing have been produced – all within optimum flow range. These stories span over nearly 10 years and different times of the year, with one thing being consistent and that is optimum flow range.

I was already researching optimum flow range when we had a late flood that dragged into October. Normally this area is good in the early part of the year. But what about late in the year during optimum flow? I pulled in to test the spot and within one minute of putting bait down was catching fish. The area held fish, even in the fall until the flow decreased below the optimum flow range and the catfish migrated back downstream.

This is the fish that hit within one minute of setting lines in a fall optimum flow range bite. It was 36 inches long and weighed 21 pounds.

According to research on the Red River of the North, the optimum flow range is usually reached after a flood or near a high-water event. The optimum flow range is normally at about 75 percent of flood stage. On the Red, that's 28 feet. Other possible reasons optimum flow range may provide some of the best fishing of the year is during the spring as the runoff is winding down. This is particularly true in a northern river system. This is also at the same time when the metabolism of catfish is rising with water temperature. We will visit this aspect of fish biology and their behavior later on in the book.

SECONDARY CURRENT

You cannot write about flow range without discussing high water and what happens to the fishing when high water occurs. As pointed out in Chapter One, focusing on the secondary current is the key to high water fishing success.

A secondary current is formed when a river reaches a high point and creates two outside channels that extend from the now flooded shoreline to the main current. The water next to shore is moving at about half the speed of the water in the main channel. Think of it like this: the river has broken into three rivers. The main channel becomes its own river in the center where most of the flow is moving at a high velocity. The two outer rivers are moving at about half speed and are on the outside of the main channel along the banks.

It is important to note that all the high water debris, such as tree branches and other flotsam, will always flow in the main channel. When the river is high enough to break into the three channels, you can run a boat in the outside channels with ease, avoiding the debris in the middle.

When a river breaks into these three channels, the catfish want to swim in the main channel about as much as you want to anchor the boat and fish in it. They want to follow the path of least resistance and that's along the break lines where the secondary current is formed or along the shallow edges of the secondary current. Later on I will introduce you to lateral movement. With a little understanding of lateral movement you will unlock the door to catching catfish in the secondary currents during high water events.

In 2005, we were elated to finally – finally! -- have our brand new boat ramp open in Grand Forks, North Dakota (that's another long story). It was early May and cabin fever was in full force. The fishing itch needed to be scratched. Like we have for many years, I launched the boat with a friend and headed north, down river (the Red River of the North runs from south to north). The flow was way too high to anchor mid- river so we were forced to fish along the banks. We had a great day and landed many big fish. At the time, we still did not understand why we were fishing the way we were other than to not get hit by debris. We did not fully understand why we caught fish in the secondary current until years later.

The very next season (2006) we started out catching huge fish. We were still trying to fish mid-river whenever we could but due to floating debris we were forced to fish along the bank yet again. Action was fast, but we still did not understand what we were doing and why the fish were reacting the way they were.

One similar day during the pre-spawn, my friend emailed me saying members of the local catfish league had some success near the boat ramp the day before. We got the hare-brained idea to take a long lunch from our jobs and go fishing. That lunch hour, after only a few spot changes, produced 12 catfish with two heavier than 20 pounds! And we did not leave sight of the boat ramp.

Noontime Channel Cats

Fast forward to the spring of 2008; it was not even close to the same as 2006 in terms of spring flood intensity. I just had to find out if the secondary current pattern would work again like it had in '06. We anchored, baited and started fishing one of our traditional hot spots. The fish were there just as they had been two years earlier. It took about a minute for me to realize the fish were running the break line and fishing was going to be awesome. That first day was just a taste of what was about to come later that week.

2009 presented yet another huge flood. When we finally got into the river and hit the tried-and-true spots, we couldn't find fish. What the heck, I wondered, where were the fish? After further research the fish had not moved into the traditional spring locations because flows were still far above optimum flow range. Rather than wait for the fish to show up, I fished downstream in more traditional spots with success. As the weeks went on, the fish seemed to be biting closer and closer to the traditional spring hot spots. Finally, one Wednesday night everything came together. The fish were in the zone just like they had been the previous year feeding along the current breaks. The bite lasted about two weeks before the fish moved off to spawn.

It was not until the next year (2010) when I thought I might be able to predict the bite. The prediction was almost right on target based on river conditions. Many anglers base good bites on the calendar and not the conditions. The calendar is only a basic guide. River conditions and seasons are the true indicators of catfish behavior. With conditions nearly identical, the bite turned on but it turned off almost as quickly.

This is a secondary current seam. The water tells exactly where the break line is from the main channel to the normal shoreline. Just look at the flat water to show the exact point of the break line.

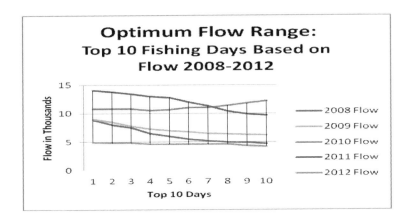

The chart above shows optimum flow range window over five seasons. This illustrates that the flow is always within range and fairly stable.

So what happened to cause the bite to shut off so quickly? What led to these awesome bites and quick turn-offs? With just a little research, it quickly became obvious that an optimum flow range existed during the best fishing action, just as the records in four of five seasons showed. Even after this realization and with a few more seasons under my belt I'd proven the pattern was no fluke two more times. One year had the river exceeded optimum flow range in the pre-spawn and the next year the flow range was reached for about a week. We caught fish and proved the pattern yet again.

What made this pattern so successful was that the flow was in the optimum range and coincided with the pre-spawn season. Channel catfish tend to move upstream to feed and prepare for the upcoming spawn season. What made this area so great within the optimum flow range is that the catfish were on the feed just below a dam which was bottling up the catfish forcing them to feed and move within that flow until it was time to head out to the nest to spawn.

This theory has also been proven on another stretch of the Red River of the North during two other seasons. Again the fish were feeding in the pre- and post-spawn while the river was in optimum flow range near a dam. In both cases, the area was hot and heavy when within the optimum flow rate. However, fishing did shut down when the flow rose above optimum and also when the flow went below optimum.

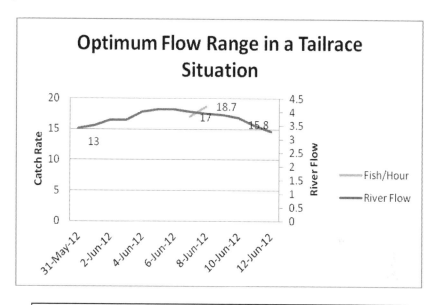

This graph explains how a tailrace can be fantastic when the river is in optimum flow range. When optimum flow range has been established you can see where tailrace situations can have great fishing.

CATFISH TIP- Be careful when fishing in a tailrace to avoid the center boil and the back eddy outside of the current seam. Losing control of your boat in these spots can spell disaster.

FINDING THE SECONDARY CURRENTS

Once you figure out what the break lines and secondary currents look like from a water perspective, they quickly become obvious. Usually the main channel breaks into the secondary where the original shore line meets the current of the main channel. These secondary rivers are not as straight and winding as the main channel in normal conditions. There are wide spots and narrows spots depending how the river behaves.

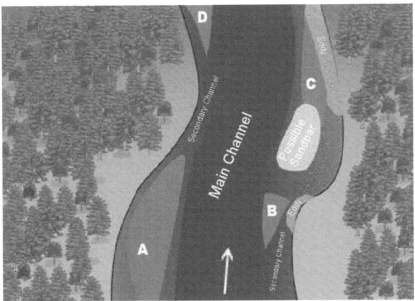

Graphic Provided by Iowa Sportsman Magazine

The graphic is a great example of secondary current and how a river breaks into three rivers. You can see the main channel and where the two outside rivers form. These secondary rivers provide all of the same structure as the main river during normal flows. You can see where right before the river turns and a back of an inside corner (B and D) create a true secondary current that runs about half the speed of the main channel. As the main current goes by, it drops food in the secondary, making for easy catfish meals.

There are also secondary currents that can form just before the outside corner, behind sandbars or some other structure. A and C explain where these seams might be.

During times of low water, you can see where the secondary channels run based on the bank composition that is now dry land. There are outside bends of a river that have the bank literally torn apart and jagged. This is a sure sign that during high water conditions the river will pound into that bank on the turn and tearing apart everything in its path. Another giveaway is that way up on the bank there is sometimes a large pile of driftwood that has been thrown from the main channel as it turns the corner. In northern rivers, these banks may have sheared off tree stumps or trees where the bark has been torn off by sheets of ice.

The photo of the far bank shows what happens when hard flood waters push up on the bank. It creates a steeper cut bank and tears out the trees and other vegetation.

Conversely, the areas where the secondary current forms are the spots where the bank is very smooth and soft on the cut bank. This shows that the energy of the main channel has avoided the area. These secondary channels are what you should focus on during high water.

This photo shows the soft side of the river where the secondary current seam leaves a gradual slope and can deposit a sandbar/point.

After learning how to visualize and understand the concept of three separate rivers during high flows, it is time to start thinking about the secondary as its own river. Once you have achieved this feat you will realize that the secondary river fishes just like the main river in normal conditions.

Within the secondary river you will find snag piles, underwater sandbars, troughs, and of course, holes. This is the point where just simply looking and learning the lay of the land comes into play. Consider it as learning a new river or a bonus river.

There are some spots that you can look for to speed up the process of learning the secondary channels. The first and most obvious is the back of an inside bend. As the main channel makes a turn it usually plows into the outside bank. When this happens just at the outside of the turn on the inside corner you can actually see a "V" formed on the water. This "V" is basically dead water between the main current and the eddy located along the bank as the main channel ushers the water downstream.

This shows an almost perfect "V". If you look closely you can see where the main current comes around the corner and the riffled part is the higher point of the inside bend which causes the secondary seam and hence forms the "V".

When the water is storming past the corner, it is dropping food into the "V" just as if it were a big snag on a bend during normal conditions. Anywhere in this "V" can hold fish but there are so many more locations off the inside bend that may have hungry channel catfish waiting. As stated earlier in this chapter there is a soft drop off that is the home of the secondary current. These soft drop-offs provide running channels for high water channel cats. In many cases they are carved out over time creating one to three foot drop-offs. These drop-offs provide the perfect fish highways depending on what the flows are.

Here you can see how a secondary would be formed in a high water event. Imagine another 15 feet of water in the river. Right were the shoreline meets the water would create a secondary seam.

Another great spot to find the secondary current line is along some river straight aways, or even just before or just behind outside bends. Outside bends that have big, jagged edges torn out are not the home of secondary currents, but there are spots near the cutouts where perfect secondary currents are formed.

The easiest of these currents to find is right after the main channel turns the corner and points to wherever it is going to head. Sometimes after it makes the turn and returns to the main channel it creates a secondary current toward the backside of the outside bend.

Another spot that is sometimes harder to find in high water is the secondary that can be formed right before the outside bend. These particular spots are usually formed because, in normal conditions, there are sandbars under the water. The sandbar acts as a current break and will hold fish. The fact that there is a sandbar in the spot tells you that the current is slow enough to drop silt and deposits to create the sandbar in the first place.

The two photos above tell a very interesting story about how a sandbar affects currents. The top photo was taken during low water and clearly shows a sandbar that has formed. The bottom photo shows the same spot during high water and you can see the secondary seam that is created -- and it holds catfish.

If you study the river bank and understand them you'll notice that beavers always build their houses on the secondary current spots. They do this in areas where flooding will have the least impact on their house allowing it to survive that spot. Beaver houses are also a great indicator of the secondary current spots.

Fishing these secondary areas from the current break to the bank in high water can make the difference in catching more fish versus just fishing the old standard holes or log jams. The only way to find these spots and understand them is to be on the water and study them.

The last of the spots to look at in the secondary channels are the most obvious and not always available to fish. This can be a great opportunity to fish some of the snag piles that are formed when trees fall from the bank but have remain rooted and stuck in the bank rather than falling into the river to be drug away later to create a snag downstream. These snags are normally visible and out of the water during low water, but they provide great hiding spots in high water.

When fishing the flooded shoreline spots in the snags, don't be afraid to fish the shallow side near the root ball. Root balls are known to hold channel catfish, especially smaller catfish but during high water can also have trophy fish take up residence.

The photo on the previous page shows a cutbank with a fallen tree just off the drop off. In high water, this spot would form a perfect secondary current with structure.

If you are fishing above a snag you should fish the shallow side of the root ball as well as the deeper side. If you can run more than two lines, make sure to cast a line or two tight into the main part of the snag as well as a line right off the break line toward the middle of the river where the secondary current forms. In this way, by covering a newly flooded snag, you can determine at what point in the current seam the fish are resting and actively feeding.

In addition to the traditional anchoring upstream of the snag and casting into the heart of it from the front, tying in tight to the back of the snag may also produce fish. The way to set up on this is to drive up into the back of the snag and tie in or use a brush grip. From there you can cast downstream, working the holes and break lines as well as fishing in the snag vertically to see if there are any channel cats that may be in the back of the snag in the boil created by the log jam.

This method can be a great way to find active catfish trying to stay out of the main current and it can also protect your boat in some marginal spots along the main river current from being hit by debris that may be floating down the main channel and putting you in an unsafe situation.

CATFISH TIP-
Things about rivers that you can learn from a puddle

Every river operates pretty much the same in terms of current and how the water flow affects structure. Snags, rocks or other debris will form holes and ultimately feeding spots that attract channel cats.

You can study how water behaves anywhere it is running. Even a mud puddle allows you to see and learn how water moves. As you watch a puddle or even street runoff you can be presented with an opportunity to learn a lot about rivers and what water does to create fishing spots. From there you will better understand how catfish relate to different spots and currents.

If you find the right area of runoff, you will see where a main channel has formed into everything a good cat man would love. It contains inside corners (current "V"), outside bends, where the secondary currents are formed, and even holes near stones and sticks that may represent snags.

By watching this flow for some time you will start to notice on a small scale where the best places to fish during certain situations and will start to realize what a bigger river will look like and what is going on as you look out from your boat or use your electronics.

Much can be learned from runoff or a puddle. So steal a moment and learn how a river really moves and lives.

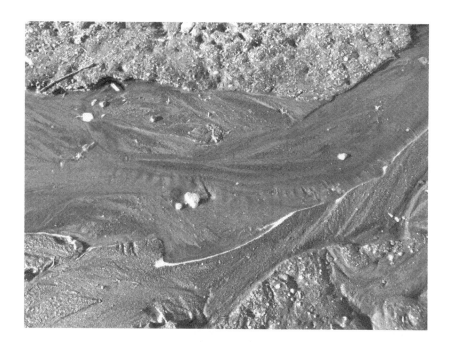

In the photo of the puddle above, the riffle of the water cuts a channel on the outside edge (bottom) and turns back. This shows the exact areas of the secondary seam. It also shows where a hole is forming with its own seam next to the rock. You can also see on the top right where a sandbar is forming but the current created a hole next to a rock.

The puddle photo on the next page shows a torn edge toward the top. This is where the fastest current tears a hole and a trough. (It would also be the location that would collect snags and debris.) On the lower side, the effect is very subtle and forms the current's seam on the secondary.

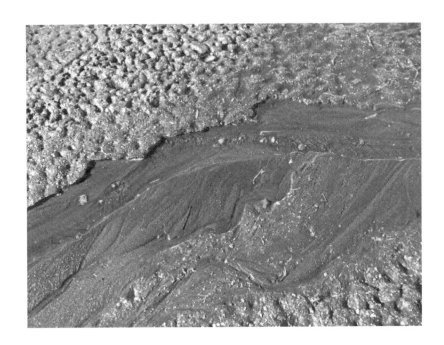

HOW FISH MOVE WITHIN CHANGING CURRENT

As a river rises and falls throughout the year, channel catfish move and migrate to ensure their own survival. Later in Chapter 11 we will discuss the seasonal patterns and how everything fits together.

Over the years there have been many tracking studies conducted on channel catfish movement. These studies have found that catfish fall into three distinct behavioral groups. There are catfish that stay very close to their home ranges and move very little within that home range except during the pre-spawn feed and the fall migration to find wintering holes. The second kind of catfish has a home range but does not stay as close to home. The third kind of channel catfish migrates great distances.

A study of the Red River by the University of North Dakota found that most catfish will stay very close to their home range most of the time. In the study, transmitters were implanted into some catfish and they were immediately returned to their home area where they were caught. The fish remained in that home area most of the season. Later the transmitters were implanted in fish at a boat ramp a few miles from where they were trapped. Upon implantation they immediately returned to the home range from where they were caught.

AN UNSCIENTIFIC STUDY

When I started researching this book, I wanted to answer the question of where catfish go when the river flow is experiencing dramatic changes with every rain shower. When trying to find fish at different water levels, I never took for granted any observation of where fish were caught or how they were caught.

The first season basically tried every location and tactic to catch fish with some consistency as the river fluctuated. Once the secondary current theory was discovered it became obvious about how these fish moved in the current. Now the question changed from where do they go with fluctuations in flow to how do channel catfish move in the other conditions.

It is widely known that in the springtime during the pre-spawn, catfish tend to move upstream feeding and preparing for the upcoming spawn and that they tend to move downstream to the wintering holes where they will live with other channel catfish in a near dormant state during the cold water times of year. This at least applies in the northern ranges.

Using this basic knowledge has made catfishing fairly predictable during the pre-spawn and the summer months but not so much during years when water conditions are unpredictable. In high water conditions and low water conditions the channel cats seem to be very elusive to many anglers.

During the first three years of research, there were water conditions at the extreme high and low levels. The simple findings indicate that when river flow was high, the fish tended to feed and migrate upstream regardless of season.

I also noticed that there were more large fish being caught farther upstream than during normal water conditions. During the worst high water season in over a three-year stretch, Captain John Dickelman from Moorhead, Minnesota, documented catching more fish weighing 15 pounds or more than in any other season in his guiding career. He caught many channel catfish tipping the scales at 20 pounds or more when, in normal seasons, only a 20 pound plus fish or two were landed.

I also documented that during high water times that fishing structure could replenish fish much quicker than in lower flows. Normally a spot cannot be fished more than a couple times per week with any real success. But when the water was high, spots could replenish with cats every 24 to 48 hours. Depending on river conditions and angler activity, spots can theoretically be fished every two to three days showing little pressure as long as flows remain high.

Besides the upstream and downstream movements, this research project took into consideration how channel catfish moved laterally within the river as water levels rose and fell with constantly changing current conditions from the main channel to the secondary channel.

Channel catfish swim the line of least resistance for food and survival in rivers. When the river is low to normal flow, all areas are free game for catfish to set up shop. As water levels rise and flow velocity increases, the fish move laterally up the break lines within the secondary currents that form along the cut banks as much as they will move upstream. The catfish will also move out of the main current seams and into areas with less current.

When flows are low, channel cats tend to stick to their home range or even move downstream in search of more favorable conditions. This research project also showed that this was the case. One thing that was very noticeable is that fishing spots took much longer to replenish. In lower flows, it can take five to seven days for a spot to replenish with catchable catfish. This means anglers must cover more water and fish more spots giving each area time to replenish.

These two channel cats were caught as a direct result of adjusting to flow levels. The fish were taken by simply looking shallow (off current) during a negative pattern. Finding the right current seam can be very rewarding.

CHAPTER 5
ANCHORING

Understanding flow is one thing,

But how do you manage flow with a boat?

Knowing how to anchor your boat in current – all types of current – is one of the most important, fundamental river fishing skills you can master.

TYPES OF ANCHORS

There are many types of anchors and they all do the same thing. Some work better in certain situations than others. The real key to using an anchor is understanding when one style works better than another. Selecting an anchor is determined by the type of river you are planning to fish, the boat's hull design, and the bottom composition of the river.

A mushroom anchor is round and has no appendages to grab bottom. Like its name suggests, it looks a lot like a mushroom. It works best in slow moving water with a mud bottom. That's because the anchor tends to frequently give way on harder bottom surfaces, especially in heavy current.

Fluke anchors have two triangle hooks that, with pressure, dig down into the bottom. These anchors are known to be lightweight and easy to let out and retrieve. They work great in sand and mud bottoms, but have a tough time grabbing hard bottom. Using fluke anchors can work in heavy current, but a longer rope is needed to prevent slipping.

River anchors are very heavy anchors that work very well in heavy current. Once they are dropped and dig in they will hold the boat tight to a spot. Their design is made to catch on hard bottom and will also work well in mud or weeds. Their downfall: They tend to be difficult to retrieve.

The grappling anchor is very effective when used with smaller boats. These anchors are small and light. Featuring four hooks that fold down to catch the bottom, they are limited to anchoring a small boat or canoe. A modified grappling anchor that's heavier and has fixed spikes can, however, keep average size boats in place. The only problem that arises with this type of anchor is that the spikes can get caught in tree branches or between rocks. And who wants to cut the rope and lose the anchor?

The last and best river anchor, in my opinion, is a cross between the grappling anchor and the fluke anchor. It has the slim, lightweight design with fluke style spikes. A connected chain completes the rig. If the anchor becomes snagged, simply moving backwards over the anchor lifts the chain and frees or bends the flukes. Problem solved.

The Cat River Anchor offers the best of everything for river fishing. It is light weight and boasts wide flukes. This allows the anchor to hold in most situations and can be easily released when snagged.

UNDERSTANDING YOUR BOAT

Your boat's size and shape dictates what size and style of anchor you'll need to use when anchoring and save yourself some headaches.

Shallow running boats are very popular among the river-running crowds, especially when the river is known to be very shallow. The words "shallow running" tells it all. Shallow running boats draw almost no water when under way and tend to sit high in the water when at rest. These attributes help them move about in the shallow stretches of a river.

The medium V-type hull is most common in today's boats. These boats sit in the water from a foot to 18 inches, depending on it's weight. The main feature of this hull is that they run smooth in smaller waves and have great control while running in moderately rough water.

A deep V boat sits deeper in the water when at rest. The V in the hull helps push water to the side when running. This feature helps these boats run smoother in rough water -- without beating up the passengers. This ability to run in big waves is not necessarily a good thing when anchoring because the hull creates more drag in current. Deep V boats will work in large rivers but may not be the best choice for running a river's shallow areas.

> **CATFISH TIP-**To avoid swaying in wind and current while under anchor, tie directly to the main cleat of the boat or add a cleat on the center of the bow.

SUCCESSFUL ANCHORING

So you have your boat and an understanding of anchor types. So what's involved in anchoring to get the boat to behave the way it must to help ensure proper presentation of bait?

Shallow-running boats tend to ride the current and get caught up in waves making it more difficult to keep anchored straight and without drifting. If your boat has a larger, flat bottom, you may need to have a heavier anchor and use more rope to keep the boat where you want it. Medium or deep V boats will need to be anchored accordingly to the size of the boats. Because the V bottom allows them to slice the current, it will hold the boat straighter in the water. This sometimes means you can get by using a smaller or lighter anchor compared with the ones required while using a flat bottom boat. Wind and other factors can change those requirements however.

How you use that anchor is the next item to think about. Rope type and length is the connection to successful anchoring. The length of anchor rope is as important as the anchor you choose to use. You should consider a 100-foot length of at least one-half inch nylon rope as the connection standard. A rig such as this will allow you to long-line in deeper or faster water.

A good rule of thumb in determining rope length is "the rule of three." That means for every foot of water you plan to anchor in you should let out three feet of rope. For example, if you plan to anchor in 15 feet of water you would let out at least 45 feet of rope. If a strong wind is blowing from the same direction as the current, you may be required to let out more rope to keep the boat in place.

Once you let out the proper length of rope, tie it off to the front eyelet or cleat at the center of the bow to keep the boat as straight as possible.

In situations where waves are smacking the boat you may be knocked off your anchor point.

To prevent this, add three to four feet of chain between the anchor and the rope. Now when the waves hit the boat the weight of the chain will lift up, but the anchor should remain in place, locked to the bottom.

There are other ways the wind can affect your ability to stay anchored in your desired location. If the wind is from the side or against the current, the boat will tend to swing. This can be absolutely maddening. Sometimes the boat will swing a few feet from side to side. Other times, the wind will blow the boat back over the anchor. In either situation, placing and keeping bait in the zone becomes impossible. When this happens, set a second anchor out the back of the boat and tie the rope vertical leaving minimum slack but enough so you don't swamp should a wave come up from behind. This will prevent the back end of the boat from the swinging. There could be a downside to this technique, however. A second anchor can make landing a fish more difficult because the fish can get wrapped up in the rope. If you don't want to take a chance with losing a fish to the rope, another way to keep the boat from swinging is using a drift sock on the back. The river's current will catch the sock and your boat will remain straight allowing you to fish the strike zone.

If anchoring with the boat facing into the current doesn't make you comfortable, there is another method. Some people prefer to side anchor. This anchoring technique is when anchors deployed off the bow and stern force the boat to sit perpendicular to the river's current. When side anchored, you cast downsteam and set all rods on the side of the boat. This method tends to keep the boat firmly in place and straight and the lines remain away from the anchor rope when reeling in fish. One major downfall to this style of anchoring is that the occupants tend to sit with their backs into the current and may not notice impending floating dangers - such as a tree - moving toward them full speed ahead. If one of these logs hits a boat or the anchor ropes, the boat could sink in mere seconds. The other downfall of side anchoring is when wind blows against the current your boat will still sway. I highly advise against side anchoring just because of line control and safety.

Everything we have already discussed in the flow chapter connects with anchoring. When anchoring on the current seams during low to normal water you will want to set the anchor on the higher side of the break. That allows you to cast into the current side and walk the baits back to the exact point of the current seam.

Should you want to fish upstream of a snag or other structure, simply set the anchor and let rope out until you are a comfortable cast from your target. Having extra rope to pay out could improve your chances of getting the bait into that hot spot.

When fishing the "V" in the secondary current, anchoring in the right location is critical to making sure you are in a safe spot and able to get the bait into the strike zone on the secondary current. Just as you would anchor in a heavy current seam, set the anchor on the high side of the break line and upstream of the "V". This will allow you to stay out of the main current and put the baits right into the strike zone.

Successful anchoring can translate into successful fishing.Understanding what style of boat you own and what bottom structure your river contains will help you choose the right anchor. Once you choose the right one for your needs and learn how to use it properly you will never have problems staying in the strike zone.

And staying in the zone equals more fish in the boat.

CHAPTER 6
BAROMETER AND BEHAVIOR

"The fishing sucks."

Heard that before?

Chances are the anglers muttering it, regardless of the fish species they were pursuing, probably were blaming the barometer more than anything for the bad bite.

It is common to hear the debate of "the barometer is too high" or "the barometer collapsed causing a bad bite." The truth is, the barometer can simply be an indicator for a pattern of what is about to happen above or below water in connection to weather.

When I first started really paying attention to environmental conditions, I tried to figure out what was driving catfish behavior. I fell into the group who bought into the "a low barometer brings on a front that shuts the fish off." I remember two specific occasions where the barometer took a hard drop and the fishing shut off.

The first time it happened, I was about to take an outdoor writer fishing. He wanted to mention me in an article that he was planning for a future issue of his newspaper. Fishing was quite good during the week considering that we were at the end of the spawn and beginning of the post- spawn. The day before the trip we had a massive cold front hit and the day of the trip was nearly 20 degrees cooler than it had been. We started fishing as normal, but there were very few fish active in the spots where they had been aggressive. We ended up catching some fish but no monsters. All I could do at the time was blame the barometer for the big drop in catching success.

The second episode happened while shooting an episode of "Catfishing America," a nationally broadcast television show highlighting the United States' top catfish destinations. We had been on fish all day and caught some nice fish for the camera. Toward the end of the day we noticed the barometer was dropping fast and we ended up being chased off the water early by a brewing storm. The next day our great bite was not so great and we had to work very hard to put fish in the boat. Both the host of the show and I insisted that the barometer had put the catfish in a negative feeding mode and we had to tough it out to finish our shoot.

During the original barometer research, I read many talk forums and made many phone calls to prominent catfish guides and tournament anglers to find out what was being said about how barometric pressure affects catfish. It was quickly evident that nobody agreed on what the barometer means to a catfish pattern. Most anglers (especially in the south) said they prefer a falling barometer over a high barometer. When you keep poking these folks enough you find that what they are saying and interpreting has a lot to do with light conditions -- that a high barometer means blue bird skies and a lower barometer equals more cloudy and overcast conditions. It's the low light and overcast conditions that the fish tend to like.

In my own fishing I always was under the impression that a barometer that was stable to high became a nonfactor for the bite. I knew that a quick barometer drop made for a tough day on the water. Yet it seemed that a barometer drop was tougher on the bite some days than it was on others. In hindsight, now I believe I was buying into the "bad barometer" idea rather than the barometer's actual effect on the fish.

It was not until the summer of 2011 when I guided Jake Bussolini, who was researching his book, "The Catfish Hunters," that the idea of the barometer having little impact on the fish really came into play. Bussolini has done extensive research of his own and says the barometer means nothing to fish and he states that he has proven it mathematically. Instead, he believes that it is the sun that influences the bite. On one hand, I choose to disagree with Bussolini that the barometer means nothing, yet, I also agree with him on the subject of sunlight.

Bussolini has an interesting take on the barometer. He claims that the change in barometric pressure when explained in pounds per square inch (PSI) is so small that it becomes irrelevant to how a fish reacts. In his book, "Beneath the Surface," Bussolini used one day as an example when the barometer rose from 29.92 to 30.04. He says that in that example, pressure changes versus barometric pressure changes at 10 feet only differed a little over 0.05 or 0.4 percent. In terms of PSI this would amount to a little less than 0.4 pounds per square inch.

Bussolini goes on to say that his theory is not so much that a change in barometric pressure alters the catfish bite patterns but that the sun has more of an impact on fish behavior. He says that fish bite better on overcast days and not as good on clear, sunny days. In other words he believes that the barometer is just an indicator of the weather in general: when it's sunny, fish bite less frequently; when it's cloudy, fish bite more willingly.

So what does the barometer actually mean to catching catfish? The barometer affects catfish, but not in the way most people think. It turns out the barometer must make a big drop to affect fish behavior. It should be noted that a slight drop such as 30.00 to 29.95 is a nonfactor -- but that a drop from 30.00 to 29.6 is a substantial change.

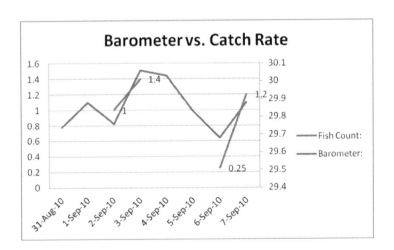

The chart above is a great example of how the typical channel catfish bite can relate to the barometer. The chart shows a week when two storm fronts pushed through and the corresponding catch rate numbers following the fronts. This acts as an indicator to fluctuations in water temperature, which can be the ultimate cause of a spotty bite.

When a drop in barometer takes place, the fish slow down, but they don't quit feeding. What they do is hunker down as the front passes. In this case a simple change in presentation is needed. To stay on the fish you must start to fish slower and less aggressively. This will be discussed in depth later in this book.

A perfect example of this happened when I was guiding Bussolini and Mac Byrum for their book, "The Catfish Hunters." On day two, a front strong enough to feel pushed through the area. We noted that the fishing had slowed some but did not shut off. Within a few hours, action was full on again just like nothing happened.

What did happen was a front indeed pushed through but it contained none of the typical stormy weather. The storm system stayed to the south of us and was short lived. We did have to make one small adjustment which was to fish a bit slower until the fish turned back on.

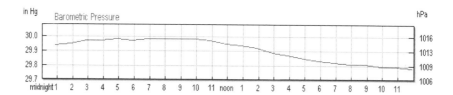

This is the barometric graph from the day with Jake Bussolini when we experienced a barometer drop. We actually felt the biggest drop between 4 and 5 p.m. By 8 p.m., the fish had moved out of the current and began feeding again.

The pattern change with a barometer drop can last as little as two hours or as much as two days. Normally when the barometer takes a sharp drop there is a storm that follows and sometimes halts fishing regardless. If you are fishing, a couple small pattern changes can make all the difference in the world. First, look to adjust your location from more aggressive spots to tighter structure and off the main current seams. This seems to combat the initial shock of a barometer drop. Second, fish slower by anchoring in your spots longer so fish can find the bait. A normal rule of thumb I've found is to fish a spot no more than 15 to 20 minutes without a bite before moving. If the barometer drops, try staying on a spot for up to a half-hour.

A changing barometer can become an indicator of whether there will be rain or sun. This is part of what Bussolini was saying in his sun theory. It all depends on what weather changes the system brings. This can determine the most important part of the channel catfish cycle and be the determining factor in the chain of life: water temperature and metabolism.

A NEW BAROMETER IDEA

While nobody really knows exactly what the barometer does to fish, many people have figured out ways to catch fish nonetheless. Proving this theory might be next to impossible but it will give you something to ponder…

We all know that fish can sense an approaching front. We all know that right before the front hits there is usually some sort of feeding frenzy.

What if the reason the bite gets tough after a front moves through really has nothing to with pressure at all and the reason the bite is slow is that the fish actually gorged themselves during the pre-front feeding frenzy? In a later chapter you will read about a catfish's food requirements. You will see that for a catfish to survive and grow it really does not take very much food to meet its minimum requirement.

For a moment let's use the human Thanksgiving Day behavior as an example. We get together with family and eat lots of great food. We eat and eat until we feel almost sick but are proud of ourselves for our gastronomical feat. We then go lay on the couch to rest and watch football. OK, so here's the piscatorial parallel -- this is very similar to what the catfish has done during the feeding frenzy. Back in the living room, now someone may walk over with another plate of potatoes. We would probably say "No" and not even move from our position. What if someone comes over with fresh baked pumpkin pie or a strawberry cheese cake? We will think for a moment or maybe a bit longer before we sit up, grab a fork and start eating. We really didn't want it but it was just too good to pass up.

To stick with the Thanksgiving metaphor, if you are at the family gathering, notice that the kids usually eat a little bit of food and want to go play with their cousins. They are hungry in a short time and start to snack and eat while the adults are still full lying on the couch watching football. This could explain why it is almost always the smaller fish that start biting first and the larger fish eat later after a storm.

This could explain why the bite gets tough and why being in the right spot and fishing at the right speed with the right bait is so important. Yes I'm comparing human to fish behavior. But is the example really that much of a stretch?

A lot remains to be discovered about how the barometer affects fishing. Just how does one go about collecting data and proving this theory on paper? When solved, if ever, we all will be able to consistently catch more fish.

CHAPTER 7
WATER TEMPERATURE

It seems in life that there are negative events that are horrible at the time, but eventually become something great down the road. One of those events was my first skunk while guiding clients. It was a cool, rainy Sunday in September. Fishing had been tough for a couple weeks but I was still managing to put fish in the boat for my customers.

I had two trips booked that day. The first trip of the day was guiding a young couple who had never caught catfish and wanted to give fishing a try. The second group had fished with me before. The day started out pretty well on smaller fish, but it was very evident that as the day went on that something was happening to the bite. The first trip ended with a decent showing and I knew the second was going to be tough. We started out with some spots that I had left alone the first trip to keep them fresh for the second.

I soon knew something was not right. What was once light bites turning into hook sets became watching still rods with no bend – not even a quiver. I have made my living as a catfish guide by moving fast and fishing hard to stay on active fish. Knowing the fish were tight lipped I fished fast, moving from spot to spot hoping to find some active fish to put in the boat. At the time I had never been skunked while guiding and did not want the first one on this day. I moved many times, changing baits and in the end ran out of time.

It was this failure that led to a long off season of thinking about what went wrong. Why did the fish shut off and quit biting? Why was I unable to put a catfish in the boat? Why is the fall bite so difficult sometimes and so awesome during others? I pondered these questions after the disastrous trip for months. I thought about how I fished, the river conditions and also thought back to a few near-skunk trips. I reviewed records from other disaster trips and all of a sudden it hit me why the fish were not biting. It became clear that I made mistakes on both of these trips. This horrible day of being skunked opened the door to me for what is one of the biggest breakthroughs in catching river channel catfish in years.

Nearly one year after the skunk trip, the same environmental trends started to rear their head again. We had a big cold front that brought on a few cooling days. This time, I was ready to combat the cold front or so I thought. I took a keen notice to the trends in water temperature and my metabolism study. I knew the bite going into the next trip was going to be tough but I had ideas and a plan this time to make a potentially disastrous day into a fair to good day.

We arrived at the river with a plan that had not been game tested. Fishing was slow as expected, even getting a few to pull the rod but not hook up. After some location adjustments we were getting action in every spot but not the action we hoped. The fish were just not hooking up. This was a positive in relation to the skunk from the year before because at least something was happening. At least we knew we were in the right spot.

This day ended with yet another skunk (the second of my guiding career if you are counting) but after this time, I knew even more thinking was in order before the next day's trip. It was a fairly long night of mulling over ideas but then it all came together. Even though I had been fishing in the right locations I was fishing fast while searching for active fish. Metabolism had dropped 40 percent in just over a week. The fish were essentially in shock. They did not need to feed as often and needed some extra time to find the bait. The next day I fished the same type of structure and location as the day before but this time I took more time in the spots. Instead of fishing the standard 15 to 20 minutes and move technique, I forced myself to sit on the spot for 30 to 40 minutes. The logic was if metabolism had dropped by almost 50 percent then the sit time should increase by 100 percent to give the fish time to bite.

It did not take but one stop to realize patience was the ticket. Mind you the fish did not magically turn on and become lights-out and providing action people wouldn't forget. This new development consistently made what could have been horrible days on the water into good days. Fishing was consistent and the fish were high quality. By understanding water temperature, how metabolism affects catfish, and making small adjustments, increase catfishing success.

Everything in a catfish life cycle is determined by water temperature and hence, metabolism. Water temperature determines the seasonal cycles from the end of winter, through the spawn, post-spawn, summer, fall and back to winter. No season progresses unless the water temperature says so.

I have taken the seasonal water temperature baseline from In-Fisherman and somewhat simplified it. Instead of cold water, pre-spawn, spawn, post-spawn, pre-summer, summer, post-summer, fall and back to winter; I tend to use cold water, pre-spawn, spawn, post-spawn, summer and fall. This simplification just seems easier to manage as the patterns really don't change that much between most of them, especially during summer pattern.

The basic seasons as dictated by water temperature are cold water, which is ice-off to 48 degrees F.
During this time, as the water warms, the fish will leave their wintering holes and begin looking for food. Catfish will feed on anything from bait fish to dead fish that are washing up from the long winter. This is a great time to find dead fish along the banks to use for bait. Or if you are prepared, you've kept some old cut-bait from the year before in the freezer. The nasty odor of the year-old dead bait may be horrific to you -- but to a hungry catfish the smell isn't like what we experience when driving by a steak house and smelling the delicious aroma of cooking meat.

As the water warms, 48 degrees creeps into the low 50s and eventually the low 60s. This is when the pre-spawn comes into play. In most parts of the country, this is the magic time. Somewhere in the low 50 degree range, a cat's bait preference changes from old rotting bait to fresh cut bait and even live bait. The metabolism is beginning to speed up at a rapid rate and the fish know it is time to feed hard and add the needed fat after a long winter. After all, it's time to spawn.

When the water temperature reaches the low 70s, the catfish move away from the aggressive feeding areas and typically head downstream to locate a spot to nest for the upcoming spawn.

Seventy to 74 degrees is the magic number for the spawn to begin. Depending on the weather and how well the water temperatures hold or rise determines how fast the progression of the spawn takes place.

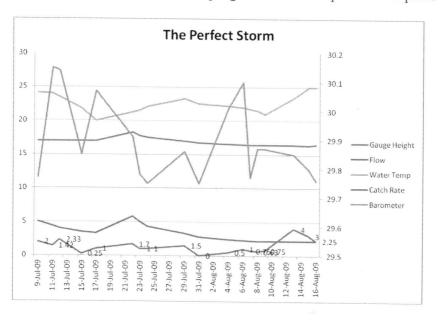

Here you can see the water temperature falls with a sharp drop in the barometer. Catch rates fall right along with it. The lackluster catch rates persisted through the unstable weather patterns and while the water stayed cool. On the right of the graph, a quick warm up shows a trigger to spur catch rates. Notice the line of the catch rate follows the water temperature perfectly.

CATFISH TIP- Every once in a while all the stars will align. Take advantage of these few opportunities by fishing aggressively to stay on fish.

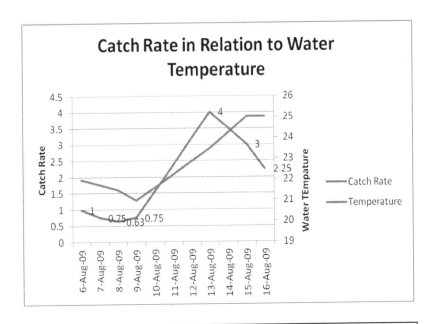

Catch Rate in Relation to Water Temperature

This graph shows stable but cool water and even cooler catch rates. As the water temperature rose quickly, so did the catch record, which spurred the progression into the summer season.

CHAPTER 8
METABOLISM

Metabolism is the set of chemical reactions that happen in the cells of living organisms to sustain life. These processes allow organisms to grow and reproduce, maintain their structures, and respond to their environments. The word metabolism can also refer to all chemical reactions that occur in living organisms, including digestion and the transport of substances into and between different cells.

> **CATFISH TIP-** Metabolism dictates everything a channel catfish does in life. Metabolism in relation to water temperature tells the fish to feed, how much to eat, to be aggressive or lay back and wait.

WATER TEMPERATURE AND METABOLISM NEEDS OF CHANNEL CATFISH

It has already been established in this book and other publications that the world of the channel cat is driven by water temperature. This in simple terms is because fish are cold blooded and their bodies have no choice but to respond to their surroundings. When water warms, fish need to eat more because their bodies are working harder to stay alive. This also means that when water temperature is cooling or cold a fish does not need to eat as much to stay alive.

When studying the metabolism of a wild channel catfish there really is not much information out there as to how it relates to fishing. However, a trip through a series of channel catfish studies that took place on fish farms provides a wealth of information and teaches a lot about the feeding needs of channel catfish.

Channel catfish farming provides decades of information on feeding and metabolism just waiting to be tapped and related to fishing wild catfish. This information is ready, available, and helps prove all of the basic metabolism theories in this book.

CHANNEL CATFISH NEEDS

A channel catfish is cold blooded and its needs are determined by the metabolic principle feeding requirements, which change throughout the year. According to a study done by the Texas Parks and Wildlife Department, channel catfish can survive with virtually no feeding when the water temperature is below 50 degrees F. This explains why in some areas (usually northern reaches) the river channel catfish almost never feed but for a few moments at a time.

In captivity when the water is 50 to 53 degrees Fahrenheit, a catfish can survive by consuming just one percent of its body weight once per week. The real feeding begins when water temperature reaches 53 degrees and rises to around 70 degrees. This is when the catfish metabolism is rising fast and fish in captivity require eating 1 percent of its own body weight at least three times per week.

For anglers who want action, 70 degrees is the magic number we're looking for. We all know that this is when the catfish begin the spawn and metabolism also begins to greatly increase at this time. When the water temperature reaches higher than 70 degrees Fahrenheit the catfish in captivity need to eat the equivalent of at least 3 percent of their body weight each day to survive and reach maximum growth. That is 700 times as much food that is required per week than when the water temperature is below 50 degrees.

Everything important in a catfish's world happens at this time. When the temperature rises above 70 degrees a wild catfish spawns, replenishes all the mass lost during the spawn, and achieves maximum growth all while being required to eat more than three times as much each day than any time of the year. It is this time when maximum catfish growth is achieved.

To put required feeding into perspective by the season, it's instructive to study what goes on at a fish farm because what happens there really amplifies the story of the catfish's food requirements. During the months of May and June, a channel catfish will eat about 30 percent of what it needs for the year. Moving through the calendar, during the month of July, a catfish needs 20 percent, August 10 percent, September 20 percent, and October into November 20 percent.

The previous numbers are a great breakdown of food requirements. Remember that catfish on fish farms are in closed environments and are fed to reach maximum potential. They do not have to deal with the daily rigors and extra energy spent on basic survival in rivers. In a study published in the Canadian Journal of Fisheries and Aquatic Sciences by David J. Rowan and Joseph B. Rasmussen, wild fish in a river need nearly double the food intake (or roughly 5 pounds of food per pound of fish per year). Eating that much food allows a fish to achieve maximum growth, recuperate from the spawn and maintain the extra energy that is required while living in the wild, fighting current and hunting for food.

Based on the idea that a catfish in the wild requires about five pounds of food per pound of fish pounds (or 150-200% of food required compared to captive catfish.) you can see using the 2012 season on the Red River to show the food requirements versus captive channel catfish.

Food requirements based on a 10 pound channel catfish

Wild: 10 pound fish x 5 pounds of food per pound= 50 pounds required

Captivity: 10 pound fish (66 x 0.3 + [3 x 12.7 x 0.1]) = 23.7 pounds required

2012 Red River (66 days above 74 degrees, 89 days between 50 and 74 degrees)

In a typical northern catfish season, the ice melts in mid-April. In May, the water usually warms up to the magic number of 50 degrees, which is the point where the pre-spawn and traditional "big" bite begins. Obviously, with fish metabolism rising rapidly (sometimes exponentially) the catfish will require most of the season's nutrients in a short time.

Water temperatures reach the ever important 70 degrees in mid-June to early July requiring a catfish to eat three times as much food daily to survive. It is during this time of elevated food requirement that one should go fishing.

Catfish farming data shows that a fish eats only about 10 percent of its year's required food in August. I think in the northern waters this time period would translate to the second half of July and first half of August. Thinking about the seasonal progression, of course a catfish would eat less during the actual spawn and post-spawn. This would explain why we see long skinny fish after the conclusion of the spawn. During this period the fish will feed even more to regain the weight that was lost during the spawn.

When catfish have completed the spawn and return to aggressive feeding to make up for the lost body mass and get ready for the cold water months, it is obvious that the fish would eat 20 percent plus of its year's required amount of food. It is also clear that the feeding would subside as the water cools in the fall as metabolism slows.

The metabolism date and information may also reveal part of the story as to why the channel catfish in the North tend to grow larger than channel cats in the south. The southern fish must eat more because of high metabolism for a longer duration of the year to survive, while the catfish in the North have a short growing season and then an extended dormant period when less food is required. Although this is my theory, it may hold some water when you consider there might be a metabolism life expectancy that takes longer to reach in cooler areas of the country while it is expedited in warmer regions.

Basically what this means is that a catfish has "X" amount of metabolism in its life. In the south, where the water temperatures are warmer, the fish's metabolism must work longer during the year to survive. In the north, where the water is cold for half of the year, the metabolism slows down for part of the year hence allowing for them to live much longer and grow larger on their allotted metabolism.

METABOLISM NUMBERS ON THE RISE

As water temperature rises, so does fish metabolism. In this research, I used an old chart provided by retired biologist L.R Schlueter to work the metabolism statistics. This chart is a simple line graph similar to the others in this book. With a little study it is very clear that as the spring water temperatures rises so does fish metabolism. In some cases the metabolism will rise by as much as 100 percent within just a few degrees rise in water temperature.

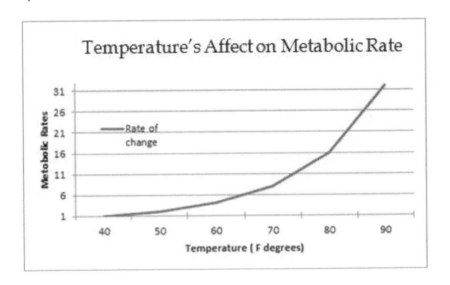

When the water of spring is in the 40s, for example, the chart gives a metabolism value of one. When the temperature reaches 50 degrees F it is given a metabolism value of two. That is a 100-percent increase in metabolism.

When the temperature rises from 50 to 65 degrees, the metabolism value grows from two to six -- a 300 percent increase in metabolism. Looking back at the feeding information from earlier, it follows that the feeding requirements have also risen nearly 300 percent. Consider that with the rise from 65 degrees F to 74, the metabolism number rises again from six to 11 signifying yet another 83 percent rise in metabolism rates. In simple terms: As the water temperature rose from 40 degrees to 74 degrees we see an 1,100 percent increase in metabolism!

This is the time in seasonal catfish progression many of us love because the hard hitting pre-spawn is in full force as the water temperature rises through the 50s, 60s, and into the low 70s. When you compare this to the catfish farming feeding charts discussed earlier it is clear why fishing is so good when the water temperatures are rising until the spawn is reached.

Metabolism charts do not stop when the water temperatures reach the mid-70s yet they show that the fish require even more food. The metabolic value of 11 is at 74 degrees. But as the temperature increases even more to 80 degrees, the metabolism values rise even faster to 16 and up again to 21 at just 83 degrees F. The rise from 74 to 83 degrees with that high of a metabolism value explains why catfishing can be so good after the spawn throughout the summer months.

In some very hot areas of the country or during a very hot year it is possible to find water nearing 90 degrees. When the water temperature increases from 83 to 90 degrees, you will see yet another metabolism increase on the chart -- from 21 to 31 -- which is another 50 percent increase. This is the time when another factor may enter into the survival equation: the dreaded dissolved oxygen levels.

DISSOLVED OXYGEN

Dissolved oxygen plays a critical piece of the puzzle in the life of a channel catfish. If oxygen levels in the water get too low, fish will experience stress and eventually certain death if levels reach a critical low point.

One of the keys to understanding how dissolved oxygen affects fish is its direct relationship to water temperature, especially when levels are low and there is little fresh water entering the system. When water temperatures are low, and the dissolved oxygen level is high, life is grand for a cat. But when water temperatures rise and dissolved oxygen levels fall a fish kill can occur. Many people think that a simple hard rain and new water entering a river replenishes oxygen. But according to fisheries biologists, this may not be the case because contaminants sometimes get into the water and quickly diffuse what dissolved oxygen there is. A fish kill is the result.

According to retired North Dakota biologist Lynn Schlueter, this sudden rush of cool water and contaminants can actually deplete the dissolved oxygen levels for a short time causing a fish kill. This is why during some drought years we hear of major fish kills happening shortly after a hard rain.

I examined six years of records in regards to dissolved oxygen for the research that went into this project on the Red River of the North. According to the catch notes and USGS data, there were no instances of dissolved oxygen depleted to the point it would kill fish. During these six years, only one time was the water temperature high enough at the same time the water level was low enough to cause any concern with oxygen levels. The catfish began to show some signs of stress, but before any significant die-off occurred there was a cool down and rain event to raise river and dissolved oxygen levels.

FALLING METABOLISM NUMBERS

You can probably guess that as the spring water warms up and metabolism increases, just the opposite happens in the fall. The water temperature decline progresses at different speeds throughout the country because of different climates.

If we work the metabolism chart backwards as late summer becomes fall, the days of course get shorter and the sun becomes less intense. If the water temperature is 80 for example, and it drops to 74, there will be a decline in metabolism of 33 percent. If it drops from 74 to 65, there will be a decline of another of 46 percent.

Just as when a fish's metabolism is rising in spring, when the temps cool it slows down at nearly the same pace. This is a time when it is critical to make the proper adjustments to stay on fish.

In the North Country, the autumn decline in water temperature can be much faster than in other parts of the country. When a fall cold front slams the region, it is common to see temperature drops of 7 to 10 degrees F over just a few days. I've already discussed how the metabolism numbers dictate the life of a fish. Now imagine the metabolism being cut by 40 to 60 percent in a matter of a few days.

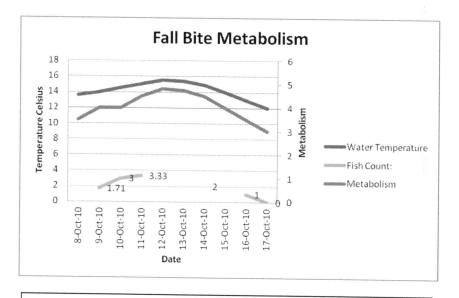

This graph indicates what can happen when there is a fall warm-up. The water temperature rises right with the metabolism. Notice in this chart the catch rates followed the metabolism as it increased but fell off as the metabolism decreased. (The decrease may have been less had the bite patterns for falling metabolic value been developed in full back then.)

Here's evidence of a strong fall bite when the metabolism value rises, turning on the channel catfish for a few glorious autumn days.

This scenario played out in 2011 and 2012 as warm summer air was jolted by cold fronts pushing out of Canada. In both cases, a huge front pushed through the area dropping the barometer and eventually bringing in cool air and rain. A few days after the front blew through, it brought cooler temperatures and cold nights and the water temperature showed a huge drop. In 2011, the water temperature fell to 60 from 69 in just seven days. This was substantial because that nine degree reduction in temperature accompanied a 50 percent drop in metabolism value. In other words, the fish went from needing to eat nearly 3 to 6 percent of body weight each day to only needing to eat 1 or 2 percent three times per week. This is a huge drop in the need to feed and hence a huge drop in catch rates.

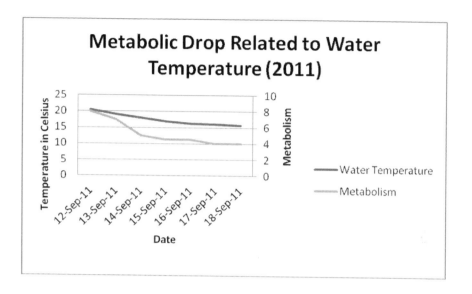

This chart shows the very quick temperature drop. Notice how the metabolism drops more dramatically as the temperature gets cooler. A fast drop like this indicates a decreased food requirement for catfish, hence slower bite.

The season of 2012 was not much different except there were a series of fronts from August through October that all led to the same basic effects as seen in 2011. In September of 2012, the water temperature fell from 74 to 65 degrees in just 10 days resulting in a 40 percent drop in metabolism. This was a very similar reduction in metabolism value to the previous year.

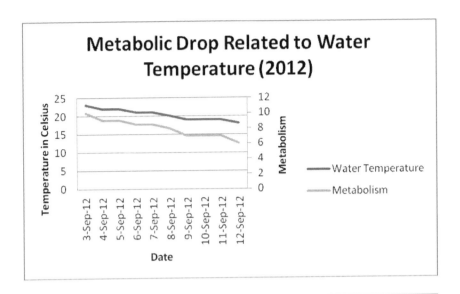

The graph above from the fall of 2012 shows a drop in water temperature (dark line) as opposed to the substantial drop in metabolism (light line). You can see that metabolism decreases at a greater rate as the water temperature decreases. Likewise below you can see the same drop happened in the summer of 2013.

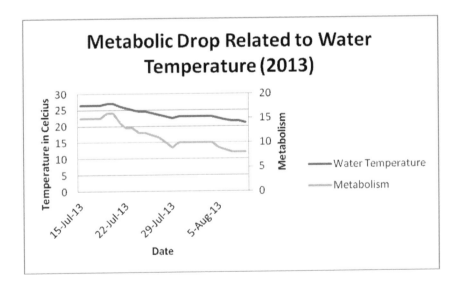

Metabolism drops in the southern U.S. are not this severe and fishing doesn't suffer compared with what happens in the North. But there are some pattern changes that come into play as the metabolism values drop in the fall. It is worth noting that just because the metabolism drops and the need to feed is reduced, catfish still need to eat and will continue to do so especially after the water temperatures level out and conditions become more consistent.

When fall sets in and starts to take hold, a decline in water temperatures and metabolism doesn't automatically drop. There are still warm snaps that happen that can temporarily raise the water temperatures a few degrees and reverse the bite pattern back to a more aggressive one.

October of 2010 provides a perfect example of this. There was a hot spell that brought nearly a week of daytime temperatures in the 80s. The water temperature had risen from 55 to 59 degrees -- a 60 percent increase in metabolism. Of course the fish responded in a very positive way. The bite only lasted as long as long as the warm up and as soon as it was over the water temperature fell back to the low 50s taking the metabolism and the great bite with it.

CHAPTER 9
MOON PHASE AND SOLUNAR CALENDAR

In all truth I have never put much thought into moon phase and its connection to catching catfish.

As a fishing guide who has to fish with customers that are scheduled months in advance, there really is nothing I can do about playing the moon phase. When I first started this research project, as I was assembling the data for the other factors, it just seemed simple to take a look at what the subject of moon phase had to show in connection with catfishing.

I had always heard or read that some of the best walleye fishing happened during the full moon night bite. After looking into it I think part of the reason the walleye guys like fishing the full moon is because it is easier for them to see and control their boat. Since this is catfish research, enough about walleyes.

Catfish guys tend to argue about moon phase, except for the flathead guys who swear the new moon period is the best for flathead catching.

Still, really knowing nothing, I entered all the data to see if there really were any trends in whether the moon phase meant anything to catching channel catfish. Since I fish according to flow and water temperature, the only analysis I have is in retrospect to see if the moon phase increased or decreased the catch rate.

What I have found in looking at six years of data on this subject is that there may be something to an increase in channel catfish catch rate at or around the new moon. Over the years, there was a very slight increase in catch rate on or around the new moon but that was only when all other factors were positive or stable.

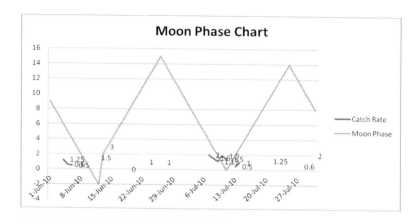

This graph (while difficult to see) shows catch rates within moon phase. The top peaks represent full moon and the bottom peaks represent new moon. If you look closely to the bottom peaks you will notice a small uptick in catch rate near the new moon.

For moon phase to truly play a role in catching more catfish, flows must be stable, water temperature must be stable to rising, and metabolism rates must be stable to rising, and the barometer must be stable. In other words all of the stars have to be aligned.

Research completed, two questions remain: Does the moon play a role in how the catfish bite? Or do the other important factors still outweigh the moon phase in cracking the catfish code? My opinion: I can say for certain that moon phase is not worth worrying about in your day to day catfishing activities.

THE SOLUNAR CALENDAR

The definition of Solunar time is the precise prediction of the rising and setting of the sun and moon.

The Solunar calendar is important to many anglers and hunters. There are deer hunters who plan their entire hunt based on the major and minor times of the day. Of all the research in this book, I've spent less time on the Solunar calendar. That's because the results are lacking and I lack interest in it.

I'm not the only skeptic. According to Jake Bussolini in his book, "Freshwater Fighters," the Solunar calendar is only 20 percent accurate meaning you will have the best success based on the calendar about one-fifth of the time. As Jake himself says "you have less than half the odds of flipping a coin." Since flipping a coin is a 50/50 proposition, this shows that the Solunar calendar is not the most accurate way to schedule a fishing trip.

For this research project, instead of using the recommended method of being in the best spots during the best times, I chose to fish like I normally do, working the pattern of the day and if a spot falls into the major or minor times, we would see if the Solunar information translated into better fishing. It seems when they tell you to be in your best spot during the "best times," we found that the key was more to be in a quality spot that was producing fish rather than concentrating on that "best time."

To get the Solunar data, I fished an entire season and tracked the number and time when fish were caught. Then I looked back to see if there was any correlation between the Solunar calendar and the catch rate. It did not take long to discover the Solunar calendar made no difference in catch rate.

My hard core conclusion is that paying time and attention to moon phase and Solunar calendar is basically a waste of time and attention. There is no need for the channel catfish angler who fishes rivers to bother following either of them.

For most people, getting the opportunity to go fishing is a challenge in itself. When the opportunity presents itself, go fish! Have fun. And use the other information in this book that has been proven much more important to creating a successful outing.

CHAPTER 10
LATERAL MOVEMENT

For many years, the fall was either an amazing time to catch channel cats or a time I just hated. It always seemed to be the best of times and the worst of times with very little middle ground. As a guide who has made a career by fishing aggressively, a typical, tough day was running and gunning, and eventually I'd find active fish.

While shooting a television show, for example, I also chose to fish aggressively -- with little to show for it. The previous week the water temperature and metabolism had taken a big dive. At one point we set up and did some cut-away shots and ended up staying on the spot for a longer time than usual. After a long sit, we started to catch fish -- nice fish -- and one from the real shallow side of the anchor spot. We moved to another spot that looked just as fishy and was notably shallow. We set the lines and started to do some more cut- away video causing another long sit. All of a sudden the shallow side of the spot started producing fish.

It took some thought after this experience to realize that two things were at play in this situation. First, sitting on the spot longer allowed slower fish to find the bait; and moving out of the traditional fishing spots and into the shallow water helped find active fish. What part of moving to the shallow side made the fish bite on this day versus any other day? Was it a fluke or did something force the fish to move? I fished to find the answer.

For decades now it has been established that channel catfish move upstream and downstream through the seasons and during changes in current. One thing that has never been looked at, except in my unscientific study, is the lateral movements that catfish make within a river.

The channel catfish tracking study by Jamison L. Wendel and Steven W. Kelsch from the University of North Dakota did a great job of explaining how channel cats tend to have a home range and also explained when catfish move up and down stream.

In an interview for this book, Dr. Steven Kelsch, one of the co-authors, was asked if they looked at lateral movement within the river. He stated that they had not looked at it during their study, first, because it was not part of the question they were asking for the project and, second, because in 1997 radio telemetry equipment was not yet combined with GPS technology to be accurate enough to show lateral movements within a cross section of river. The study done by Wendel and Kelsh helped lay the groundwork for the lateral movements determined in my nonscientific study.

The way to fish for catfish that have moved to the sides of a river is pretty simple. It comes down to making very small adjustments to your bait placement within the river. If you divide a river into a cross section with its width, rather than focusing on upstream and down, it's easier to visualize lateral movement.

Imagine a 200 yard section of river where you've traditionally had consistent action through the years. Within that section there is probably a hole, a snag or two, a trough possibly connecting two holes together, a flat and of course the shallow area near the bank -- even spots that create secondary currents. This is everything a channel catfish loves and needs to achieve comfortable survival.

HOW LATERAL MOVEMENT WORKS

Imagine when conditions are the best and fish are feeding at the head of the hole or feeding aggressively in the trough area where the current is faster. When the fish wants to rest, it can go to the bottom or back of the hole or into the snag to escape the current. Should a storm front hit, it may cool the water putting that same fish into a negative feeding mood. Then it will leave the aggressive current areas and look for somewhere more suitable to kick back and wait for improved conditions. During this time, the fish will probably not move up or downstream -- but it probably will move laterally to a snag on the edge of the hole where there is less current. Or it could move to the shallow water along the bank where it can sit using as little energy as possible.

These illustrations explain how lateral movement works and how to set your lines in different situations to catch more catfish. On the left is a situation where the metabolism is falling and the catfish moved out of the main current to the shallows (1-3 feet). The right one explains what happens with a stable or rising metabolism. This is a case when the angler should concentrate fishing the more aggressive current break, trough or hole.

When the negative conditions become positive feeding conditions, the catfish will move back out of the shallows from the slack water to the more aggressive feeding and living area within the river channel. **Utilizing lateral movement can save valuable time and fishing effort within proven areas rather than moving to other sections of river to find feeding fish.**

Lateral movement also comes into play in many other situations throughout the year. During the spring cold water time as metabolisms increase, catfish will feed in the shallow water picking up dead fish and food left over from the winter. They also like this shallow water because the mud under the water out of the current is warming the water and increasing the need to feed.

During the summer when catfish are very predictable within holes and snags, lateral movement does come into play in the same ways. The fish take up their home territory feeding and living within the best holes or snags in a section of river. Many fish feed aggressively at the heads of holes and outside edges of large snag piles, but when a weather front or cold front moves in, it can slow the bite making the fish move out of the current and up to the cut banks.

With fall approaching and water temperatures taking a quick dive, catfish will also move out of the current or holes laterally to the shallows. This allows them to dodge the current and use less energy and to use the ever decreasing power of the fall sun to soak up whatever heat there may be.

Catching catfish in high water is the most important time to understand lateral movement. When river levels rise and the currents break into the three rivers and create secondary currents, catfish may make a lateral movement to feed and rest.

Keith Sutton told a story about how in Arkansas, when the rivers flood, the best fishing happens in the trees outside of the actual river channel. The fish eat crayfish that have vacated the river to escape the high flows. The fish simply followed the food sideways to more favorable conditions for both fish and prey.

Researchers Wendel and Kelsch also noted on the Red River that during high water situations they tracked the catfish to shallower upstream water. When fish were gutted for analysis, they were full of night crawlers. This was the same situation in Arkansas except the catfish moved shallow to feed on night crawlers that were trying to escape drowning from the rising water.

Sometimes traveling long distances to catch catfish is not as necessary as some may think. So understanding how the catfish move laterally within the area they call home may be all it takes to catch fish. Of course with a high water event, some fish will make an upstream movement or even swim into a tributary until the flows subside. Just remember to look to the sides and slower current before you make that long move.

Lateral movement is an aspect of channel cat fishing that is ripe for exploration. The key is to find catfish within their home range and probe the river's sides more often. Sometimes you will make catching catfish with consistency much easier.

DAYTIME vs. NIGHTTIME CATFISHING

Catfish bite at night. This is true no matter where you fish.

Years ago, most catfish anglers were content to be shore-bound. These shore fishermen would set up camp, light a fire and cast bait into the water… and wait. During the night, catfish move out of their hiding places into the current seams and flats actively seeking their next meal. They find the bait and it's game on.

During the day, these shore fishermen could wait for many hours between strikes because the fish feed less or are in a different river location.

Channel catfish can be caught all day long.

The key is understanding their feeding and resting habits and putting the bait in front of their whiskers rather than waiting for them to come and find it. This is much easier when fishing from a boat as you can set up precisely near structure and cast right to the fish. Moving and keeping bait fresh in the catfish holding spots is a very effective and rewarding way to fish.

WATER CLARITY

Water clarity does play a role in how and where channel catfish hunt. While there has been little research done thus far on this subject, it is very evident that if water is stained, contains heavy silt, or is being stirred up by wind, channel catfish will feed in shallower water and in most traditional spots. They will also tend to actively feed during the day and at night. Light penetration or the lack thereof can dictate what break lines catfish are using or if they will hole up deep or in other types of structure.

Should the water be clearer, channel cats tend to move to deeper current breaks and holes to feed during daylight hours during certain times of the year. If the water is clear, catfish will need to be targeted tighter to structure or just in the deeper water. One way to tell where channel cats will or won't be in clear water is where sight feeding fish such as walleyes, bass or pike are holding. If the water is clear, some traditional catfish spots will all of a sudden hold other species. When these feeding fish take up residence, it is an indicator that the cats have moved to other areas of less light to hole up and feed.

Water clarity was a fairly new concept to me as it was considered pretty much irrelevant for many years. One spring, for example, there was no flood and very little spring rain fell. The water looked weird for lack of a better term and after a couple hours of looking at it I realized it was incredibly clear for May. By clear I mean there was nine to 10 inches of clarity versus the typical two.

I was fishing all my traditional spring patterns and spots but was not catching channel cats like I had become accustomed. Instead I was catching walleyes and pike in those spots. It suddenly hit me at the time that I tended to fish fairly shallow near the secondary currents in spring. But that year, with the incredible water clarity, the other fish that sight feed had taken up residence there.

The key to finding the big catfish then was to fish deeper during the daylight hours of high sun and key on more traditional spots during low-light days, windy days, and at night. After just one good rain shower, the turbidity of the river increased, clarity fell to about two inches, the walleyes and northern pike bite slowed and the catfish moved back to more normal pre-spawn locations.

When the sun is at its most intense, usually during the months of May, June and early July, pay the most attention to how catfish relate to water clarity. During these times they typically tend to hold in deeper holes and tighter to snags in the shallower areas. Should the water be fairly clear, channel catfish may more readily feed at night versus during the daytime. As the intensity of the sun weakens in late summer and fall, water clarity is less of a factor whether catfish feed during the day or at night.

CHAPTER 11
PUTTING IT ALL TOGETHER

CHARTING CATFISH PATTERNS NEAR YOU

So far we have looked at the major factors that affect the movement and behavior of river channel catfish.

Now is when some homework will be assigned to make the information all come together.

The first thing you need to do is to commit to your own data collection. If you have been keeping catch records and environmental data of your fishing trips, you are already steps ahead of the competition. If you have not kept any data from your fishing trip, this process will take a bit longer but is still easy to accomplish.

When you go fishing from now on keep a daily calendar. Keep track of how many fish you catch, how many hours you fish, and note info on the barometer, water temperature, and average water depth. Also, make a short note or two each day about what pattern worked best (or didn't work at all).

This is an example of the basic daily records I keep. Most water and weather data can be accessed and confirmed online.

If you have an connection and a reliable USGS river gauge located near you, collecting data is much easier to do. The data helps develop trends. Most gauges only have river level and flow available, while others might contain water temperature. Having a local gauge or one near you containing water temperature data makes the process of figuring metabolism trends much easier.

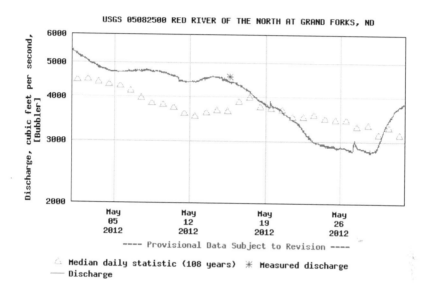

Here's an example of a USGS river flow chart. You can quickly see how the river flow trends over the course of a month. In this case it is May with fairly low flow as the river falls. At right, the rise reflects runoff from a recent rain event.

The graph on the next page shows gauge height for a month with a massive rain event pushing the river to near flood stage in just over a week. On the water, this is when secondary current seams will be forming and fish will be moving into them to feed.

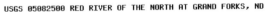

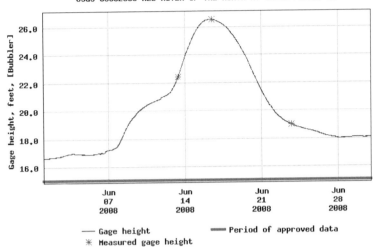

USGS 05082500 RED RIVER OF THE NORTH AT GRAND FORKS, ND

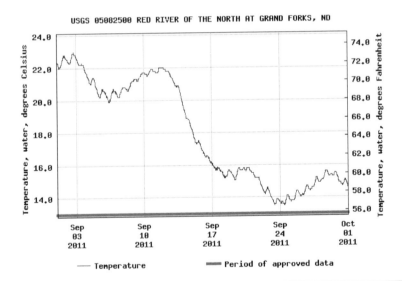

This graph shows a dramatic drop in water temperature. When combined with a metabolism chart, the information suggests fish will react and likely move laterally in the river. The angler's response: fish slowly and offer bait out of the current.

With the , you can also easily find the weather conditions for any past date you need. The best one I've found is www.wunderground.com. Scroll down to history data, enter your zip code and from there pick a day, week, month, or even a year you want to analyze.

Lastly, use the metabolism chart below to cross reference on a chart with your water temperature data. You may want to develop your own chart for ease of use rather than trying to pinpoint each temperature on the provided graph.

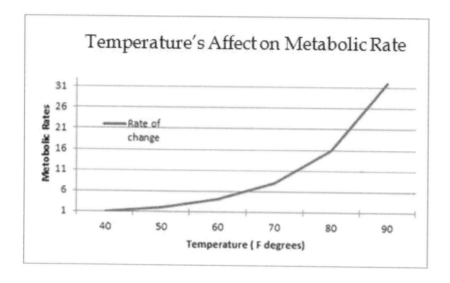

The chart above explains how fish metabolism rises with increases in water temperature. Likewise, when water temperature drops, the metabolism falls in the same increments.

Congrats! Now you know what data to collect. Simple, eh?

The next step is to build a graph to explore trends. Microsoft Excel is a great program to use for storing and graphing data. The basic setup for a graphing system is to label (give it a title) the columns with the parameters reading "date, gauge height, flow, water temperature, metabolism value, barometer, moon phase, catch rate," and anything else you would like to track.

The total number of fish caught each day should be broken down into fish per hour to stay consistent with shorter versus longer trips. Over time, this will give you a more accurate accounting of catch rates. This is done by dividing the total number of fish caught by the total hours fished.

EXAMPLE: 16 fish caught during a 6 hour fishing trip: 16/6= 2.67 fish per hour

It may take a year or two to obtain enough data to establish the desired results for trending bite patterns and determining what the optimum flow range is for your river. In the short term, you will be able to begin trending some of the patterns we've already discussed in previous chapters and when we explain them further in this chapter.

Once you get a few weeks of information together using flow, water temperature, metabolism value, and barometer you will begin to see trends, For example, when a front moves through the area, how the water temperature fluctuates and what the feeding needs of the catfish are. With this little bit of information trended, you will begin to see how patterns change and you will be able to adapt to the fishing conditions. Over time, seeing the trend and making the adjustments will become automatic and you should be able to increase your catch rates.

SEASONAL PATTERNS

So far, we have discussed how various factors affect channel catfish that call rivers home. You've learned how to adapt the information to your river. Now it is time to put that ammo into action and catch more fish as the season progresses from spring to winter. This is where the understanding of river conditions comes into play. Many will find some of this to be fairly elementary on most levels. But some of these techniques in predicting the bite are far from elementary.

SPRING (COLD WATER)

Spring can mean different things in different parts of the country when it comes to channel catfishing. The end of the cold water is when water temperatures reach 40 degrees plus. When the spring sun starts warming the river during normal flows, the fish metabolism is very low yet catfish still want to feed. With every warming day and every rising degree, metabolism increases and so does feeding activity. Even a rise from 40 degrees to 50 can kick a springtime channel catfish into high gear as its metabolism increases up to 100 percent.

During this rise in temperature, try targeting cats very aggressively using a combination of old, smelly baits and fresh baits to see which the fish prefer on any given day. Pay attention to how the flows are moving. Work the break lines near the edge of the main current seams. You should be able to work spots in a 15-20 minute pattern when the temp is rising. But you may have to slow down to a 20-30 minute sit when the water is cooling.

Catfish are still not requiring much food -- as little as one percent of body weight once per week to get by -- so if action is not producing what you want, you may have to get out of the current and work secondary current structure with longer (20-30 minute) sit times. Slow down and let the fish find the bait. Each day is different during this time of year so fish the patterns until you find what works.

During high flows, as long as the river is safe for boating, catfish can actually be easier to find than in normal to low river conditions. During a high water situation in the spring's cold water, look for feeding fish in the secondary currents along the shoreline. This is the area where the water is moving slower than the main channel or in some cases, so far off the channel in dugouts or shallow snags, that you are fishing in as little as one foot of water. The fish are still feeding but they have moved off traditional locations to avoid heavy currents. Once you find fish, you will see great results. This is a great time to focus on the "V" to see if there are fish waiting for an easy meal.

Some other spots to look at during high, cold water times are tributaries and stream inlets. Catfish will look for the warmer water to feed and these may be just the spots to head off fish as they get started in the spring progression of feeding. This is also a great time focus on tributaries because they offer cats easy pickings.

Spring is a period when catfish are still scavenging for baitfish and other organisms that have died during the winter months. So use the last of your previous year's frozen bait. The stuff can be a winner. Other baits that may work well during this time are manufactured stink baits or even sour baits such as ripened white sucker or goldeye.

PRE-SPAWN (50-70 DEGREES FAHRENHEIT)

When water temperatures stretch above the 50 degree mark and reach into the mid-60s, things really start to heat up -- literally. You have already learned in the metabolism chapter that fish are now on a mission to eat. And metabolism doubles again as the water temperature approaches 65 degrees. The feeding continues to get more aggressive all the way to the beginning of the spawn which is 70-74 degrees.

As long as the barometer and weather patterns remain stable and the water temps are stable to rising, you will be able to fish very aggressively. This is the time when you want to fish the river channel catfish along the fast water break lines, the heads of holes and even tailrace locations.

Fish are ravenous now. There is more food intake during this short time than any other period of the year with as much as 30 percent of the season's food intake being ingested. If you find a trough or feeding highway along a current seam that is showing fast and furious action, you can anchor and sit on it all day in some cases, just waiting for aggressive fish to move in and take the bait. While this is not always the best plan, when it is working, speed fishing for channel cats can come into play. Once your lines are set, you will usually know if there are active catfish within two to three minutes.

Anchoring for 15 minutes without a bite is about the maximum time to sit before moving on to the next spot. Stay on the move and you will eventually strike gold -- catfish gold.

There is one exception to this rule that may be worth using and you will know fairly quickly if it works. Sometimes when the pre-spawn is rocking, you will find yourself in the middle of lulls in the action, right after a run that has produced numbers of big fish. Instead of moving quickly after 15 to 20 minutes you may want to stay put in anticipation of another group of fish moving through on the feed. You may experience a 15 to 30 minute lull and be back in the game within a short time.

Pre-spawn is also a time when understanding optimum flow range can work to your advantage. If the river flow is within the established flow range, it is a great time to work troughs and current seams between holes and snag piles. This is where it is very important to read the current break and find the seams that are creating the highways. Once you locate the seam and visually see the current lines you can utilize a straight line pattern where law permits multiple lines.

Straight line catfishing in the pre-spawn is when you set up your boat on the outside (bank side) of the seam and cast your lines 45 degrees toward the middle of the river from the boat to the faster water then walk the bait back to the seam. By walking the baits back to the seam, the current will settle the bait into the sweet spot of the current break where there is virtually no current for the fish to swim against. These seams are locations where two currents come together and almost cancel each other out forming a "tunnel". The "tunnel" effect is a long-taught pattern promoted by In-Fisherman for many years. Most fish will be running this "tunnel" almost like a line on a NASCAR track. With all the baits in the zone of the highway you maximize opportunity. When a catfish strikes the bait, the fish will turn and swim into the faster current and out of the next line of baits. While fighting the fish, you simply transfer the other rods from their holders and your fish will stay in the main current and come right to the boat. The bonus when this happens is you will have very few issues with tangling lines.

Straight line catfishing, as seen above is when you set all lines down one seam by casting each line a little farther than the last allowing all lines to sit on the same current break in a "straight line."

A tailrace is also a great area to find pre-spawn catfish when conditions are right. As the water washes over the dam and leaves the area of the boil it creates two distinct current seams or "tunnels". (Larger dams create more seams with each gate.) If you can safely anchor the boat near one of these seams, you can create a near straight line set along the seam where the catfish will be feeding aggressively in and out of the tail race area.

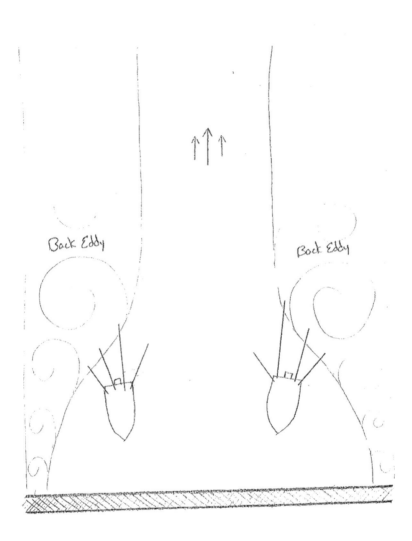

Back Eddy

Back Eddy

Above is a tailrace. In a traditional tailrace when the water rolls over the dam and straightens back out it creates distinct current seams and boils. If you can anchor just on the fast water side of these seams and get bait in the created current tunnel you may experience some of the best fishing. When fishing near tailrace areas **PLEASE BE SAFE!**

The second time I saw the pre-spawn bite arrive at gangbuster proportions on the Red River, all of the pre-spawn factors were in high gear. The river was flowing within the optimum flow window and the metabolism rates were rising almost exponentially over the course of a few days. The fish were feeding as hard as they could to put on weight and get prepared for the looming spawn that was approaching with each passing day.

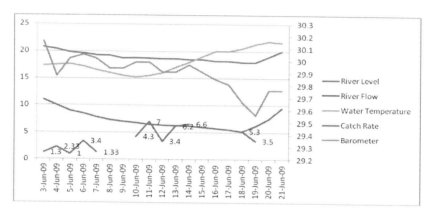

This graph shows a perfect stretch of pre-spawn fishing. At the beginning, all of the lines (conditions) are very stable with very little movement. The point is, when water and weather conditions are stable to slightly rising, the catfish respond in a positive way. At the end of the graph you can see the lines begin to spread apart from the trends; this is a major front that changes conditions from near perfect to needing some understanding and quick thinking on the water.

The fish were running a break line highway created by rip rap from a flood protection project and also along the original break line to the main river channel creating two perfect current seams. I was using a straight line method to catch fish. My guests and I would catch channel cats, usually two or three fish, within a few moments. We would take photos and release the fish back into the river. Usually by the time we were baited back up and lines set we had more fish on the other lines. We can fish two rods per angler on the Red.

A successful outcome of effective straight line catfishing.

After literally hours of fishing like this in only one spot, we found ourselves in a lull of sorts. More than 20 minutes had passed and I was getting ready to finally make a move. I decided to wait 10 more minutes because the pattern had been so productive, so why not? After about a 30 minute break, a new school of fish moved in and it was "game on" for a few more hours until the end of our trip. We fished only that one spot and rocked all day.

Getting this pattern to work perfectly is a rarity and it almost only occurs during the pre-spawn period. The pattern does not happen every year, but when it does fishing can be amazing. Understanding what drives this bite helped in understanding the rest of the factors discussed in this book.

Of course, as with any river there is a chance of spring flooding. During this high water, optimum flow range does not play a part in the pre spawn bite. The catfish will not congregate on the highway spots near as much but they will be aggressively feeding along the current seams of the secondary currents. Referring back to secondary currents, during high water, a river will become three rivers with two secondary channels created along the banks with the main channel in the middle.

When fishing these secondary currents during pre-spawn, the fish will run the seams tight to the bank or off the current break near sandbars. Catfish hold in the secondary current near the back of an inside corner of a river. This is referred to as fishing the "V" that was explained in Chapter 4. When the water is high and the river is broken into the three rivers, the main channel turns a corner and smashes into the outside bank. As it flows by on the inside it creates a "V" in the water -- literally. The point of the "V" is the point of dead water. As the V fans out, fish like to sit in it out of the current and wait for bait coming out of the main channel. Knowing the structure for these secondary currents is very easy to find with a little research during low to normal water conditions when structure is out of the water and visible.

One easy way to find a current "V" is to look for beaver houses. Beavers are masters at finding the area of least current to build their homes. This ensures that even in the worst of floods their homes will remain basically unscathed. This house can also offer up a great catfish holding spot during higher water times.

CATFISH TIP-The fastest way to find secondary currents when you are not totally sure what you are looking for is to anchor on the backside of an inside corner just on the high side of the drop off. Once you dial that in and see success finding fish, the secondary currents will come easy.

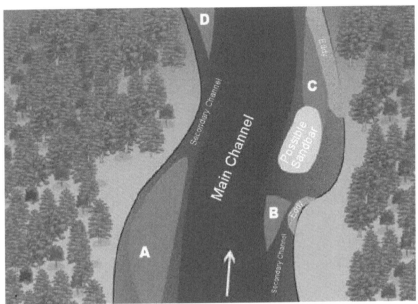

Graphic courtesy of Iowa Sportsman Magazine

The graphic above shows all the options of where secondary currents can be found. **A** is a wide offshoot of an outside corner, during normal to low water conditions it can be out off the water. **B** is a traditional current "V" right before the main channel goes around an inside bend. **C** is the back of a sandbar or other obstruction near an outside bend. **D** is a true current "V" at the back of an inside corner.

Of course there are times when all of the previously defined scenarios tend to jumble and create a maddening limbo. During this time there are no cut-and-dry answers to catching fish. All patterns must be tested to determine which way the fish are moving on a particular day. If you spend a fair amount of time on the water during an average week this will be a simple determination by testing spots that are in both patterns. It may be as simple as moving up or down the bank laterally to find the current seam that is being used during this time of transition.

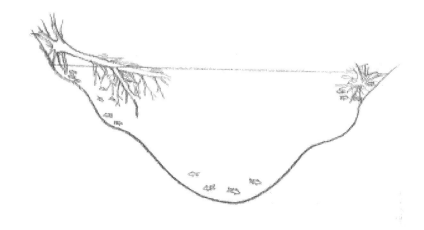

Looking back on a high water season of the past, it is clear to me how this works. On two separate occasions in the same year we were faced with near flood conditions and had been fishing the secondary currents. As the flow began to fall to the high side of the optimum flow range, it became clear that the fishing was slowing on the secondary seam. To test the system I would set up near a secondary current seam and cast two lines into the main channel break line. For a few days this was a great pattern, fishing both areas. Then it became evident that the fish quit feeding on the secondary line all together and were feeding in the main channel. So we moved to more traditional tactics of fishing in the main channel using techniques such as straight line fishing.

Conversely, when the water was on the rise we basically would follow the flows from the main channel back to the secondary seam and eventually to the "V" and also in the shallow secondary lines in as little as one foot of water.

A great example of this happened during what I always refer to as "the honeymoon trip," when a young couple spent their honeymoon fishing the Red with me. We had just come off a hard flood season preceding their trip. The pattern had just changed from fishing the secondary currents to fishing the traditional pre-spawn breaks in the main channel.

When the honeymooners arrived we went right to the main channels and began fishing the channel breaks. WOW, it was madness right out of the gate with respectable channel catfish coming at a nice rate. It seemed the fish were as happy that the water had dropped as I was. We worked the fast water and fished spots for no more than 20 minutes without a fish. This was another one of the fine bites that happened by simply paying attention to the flow rates and metabolism. Unfortunately, the metabolism study discussed in this book had not yet begun.

The happy honeymooners showing what can happen when you make a few minor location adjustments from fishing the secondary current and back to the main channel.

SPAWN

If there is a hated time of year that most catfish anglers talk about, it is the spawn period. The spawn period can be a great time or a terrible time depending on the conditions and the progression of the spawn. One thing for sure is not all channel catfish spawn at the same time or even every year. Keeping that in mind, there are always fish to catch if you simply know how and where to look for them.

During the spawn, anglers still succumb to that old adage: fish close to rocks and cut banks to catch bigger fish. The few anglers who do venture out usually fish the normal way they always do by hitting their "go-to" spots that have produced fish over the past 20 or more years. Another method they try is anchoring along steep cut banks, sit there, and wait out the fish. These strategies work but they can also make for a long day. Check that -- a really long day.

Channel cats spawn at water temperatures of 70-74 degrees and above. If the water temperature gets higher than 70 degrees and stays stable or rises, the spawn is relatively quick and painless as far as anglers are concerned. The long, drawn out process of finding and catching cats is when water temps rise above 70 for a few days then fall back to below 68. This is where understanding the metabolism values can assist you in staying on fish.

Going back to the statement that not all catfish spawn at the same time, and using the idea that water temperatures have warmed to above 70 degrees and are stable or rising, the best way to catch channel cats and especially trophy channel catfish is to fish aggressively just as you would during the pre-spawn.

Sure the number of active fish will decline a little bit as they are actively spawning. Staying aggressive and fishing break lines, deep troughs and other traditional pre-spawn spots will produce active pre-spawn fish. Eventually, as the last of the fish enter the spawning process, other fish will emerge from the spawn and start feeding to build up strength and fat after the long weeks of reproduction.

With the exception of actually being in the act of spawning, the food requirements of channel cats now are as high as they get. Remember that catfish require 4-percent to 6-percent of their body weight each day to survive and maintain, cats coming off the spawn need to eat much more than that to recover. These high food requirements coupled with the lack of feeding during the spawn explains why the mature fish look skinny and almost sickly right after the spawn. The fish are hungry now, though, and you need to employ just a bit of out-of-the-box thinking to catch the post-spawn cats. One of the easiest ways to approach the period is similar to how you use tactics in the pre-spawn period. Again, not all fish spawn at the same time.

CATFISH TIP- Remember that not all fish spawn at the same time. With that in mind, sometimes the best way to stay on fish is to just keep fishing as if it were still pre-spawn. This will allow you to catch pre-spawn and post-spawn catfish.

A few years back I was fishing fast current breaks for weeks and catching very nice catfish. All river statistics such as water temperature and flow suggested fish were on the spawn. All the other anglers were asking how I was continuing to catch fish while they were struggling. I knew the spawn was in full swing but was fishing as though it was still pre- spawn and doing very well. One Saturday, my clients and I landed 15 catfish with at least two trophies above 15 pounds and completed a great day. A day like that is a great day even during pre- spawn. The very next day, I was fishing the same pattern as the previous one but with a big difference: I did not catch one trophy-size fish in pre-spawn condition. Instead, I was landing skinny, beat up, post- spawn cats that were coming off the spawn and back to the feed. The moral of the story here is that pre- spawn ended and post-spawn had begun overnight. And the action never slowed down through the period at all.

In the photos above, the one on the left shows a catfish double from the Saturday example. These are pre-spawn fish. The fish on the right is a huge post-spawn female caught the very next day.

POST-SPAWN AND SUMMER

From the end of the spawn into the summer is a time of transition. Understanding how the fish adapt to current, temperature, and their feeding needs will play into your hand during this time.

With normal flow rates and normal temperatures, the river channel cats will move into deeper holes or snags near deeper water. Of course they will set up shop in areas that provide the easiest living and feeding conditions. These post-spawn and summer patterns are basis for traditional catfishing in terms of fishing spots and working areas to find fish. These summer patterns are best described in "Catfish Fever" by In-Fisherman. This is where the famous run-riffle-hole theory comes into play. By finding the faster moving currents and where they dump into a hole, you can find the basic home of the channel catfish. These spots are usually on a bend that possesses snags, troughs, or other barriers where catfish like to call home near or within the hole.

As the season eases into summer, the water temperature is usually fairly high, being in the mid- 70s to 80s. With water temperatures this high, feeding is a priority and the fish are willing participants. With metabolism high and the need to feed in high gear not only for growth but for replenishment from the spawn, the best way to fish these cats is to **fish fast and fish hard**. Work all the traditional spots and a few not so traditional spots. Hit all the spots and patterns staying in a spot 15-20 minutes. No fish? Move!

Fishing fast, hitting all the patterns, it will not take long to find the pattern that is working and eventually weed out those that are not producing fish. Once the pattern is established it makes fishing very quick and fun.

During the summer bite, when daytime temperatures are hot and the sun's power is at its highest, catfish will tend to sit very tight to structure during the daylight hours and be much more willing to bite during sunrise, sunset, or at night. While it is conventional wisdom that catfish hunt at night, it is only during these times of hot weather when fishing at night can be the difference in finding a bad or so-so bite and a really good bite.

I had a day when fishing fast had been very successful. I had only one client and had been on fish before the trip. We started out in the old faithful tailrace. But after 20 minutes we only had one hit and one lost fish. We moved out of the main current and in the 20 minutes that ensued we had the same thing, one hit and one lost fish. Not good.

I told my customer that we needed to make a big change so we headed downstream to a trough that had been producing fish a few days earlier and, like magic, began catching nice catfish. After an hour, the bite died down and for the next 20 minutes we did not even have a sniff so we moved. The next spot produced a few fish and then 20 minutes of dead time. The one thing I noticed after fishing a couple spots in the troughs was we would catch one or two fish quickly then maybe a third before the spot died off.

About three hours into our trip we had the pattern but were still wasting time after nailing the three fish. So we made the decision to start fishing fast and covering ground. We would stop in a spot, fish it until we caught three catfish or went just ten minutes without a bite and moved. We finished this pattern the rest of the day. When it was over we had completed an incredible day on the water and landed 18 trophy channel catfish.

CATFISH TIP- If the water is fairly clear, find deeper holes, thicker brush, or even shadowed areas to target daytime fish during hot weather.

David Howard from Virginia shows the results of what happens when fishing a spot no more than 10 minutes. Running and gunning works.

When the river is experiencing normal conditions, rotating spots is a good idea especially if you fish multiple days in a row. Some spots will cycle new fish quickly but smaller spots, especially small holes or snags, will require a few days for fish to recover or new fish to move in.

When fishing is good during the summer season, there inevitably is a large weather front that works its way through a region. We're talking cold fronts and big storms. Many catfish anglers relish the weatherman's prediction and try to fish just before the front moves in, knowing that the catfish know the storm is on the way and will be feeding in preparation. Most catfish anglers also know that after the barometer drops and the storm or cold front moves in the fishing gets tough.

This is the time that can spell disaster if you are not prepared and not willing to adjust to conditions. It might seem crazy but with a temperature drop from 74 to 71 degrees there is a 23 percent drop in metabolism and fish, of course, react to the environmental factors. During fronts, fish do slow down some but staying on the active ones is an easy fix. Simply moving to shallow edges in virtually no current near a snag or rock is all it takes. Another change that is critical is switching gears, taking more time and fishing a spot for 25 to 35 minutes. This change in temperature and conditions may seem minimal but big fish will react to the changes. This pattern can last anywhere from two days to two weeks depending on what the water temperature does. If the water temperature holds stable or rises, the fish will move back to the main channel pattern and begin to aggressively feed. That is because a fish's system recovers and when that happens they feed aggressively once again.

Back in one of the early years of my guiding career I ran into a mid-summer cool-down period at the end of post-spawn. Fishing was tough for a week and seemed to be getting worse with cold days stacked on cold days. The water temperature had fallen to 65 degrees from 70 degrees. The weather was rainy for the most part. With each passing day it seemed the fishing got tougher and tougher. I was coming off a week of bad days wondering if I had chosen the right career path.

I knew the water temperature drop had taken a toll on the bite and all we needed was some sun to warm things up. Well ask and you shall receive. The week following greeted me with three days in the mid-90s before my next scheduled trip. I headed out with some reserve, set anchor in a go- to spot and it was game on right from the start. For the next four trips with the water temps back to the mid-70s the fishing seemed easy and I was fishing most of the same spots as I had the week before. I was not just catching fish either -- they were slamming the baits with authority.

That was my first experience with a huge water temperature (metabolism) swing. When my in-depth research began years later, the trip was one that I remembered and stuck out to help me understand the patterning when dealing with metabolism's peaks and valleys. I made some mistakes and it took a success like this one to prove that fishing the aggressive pattern works in these river and environmental conditions.

Just a little warm up was all these fish needed to get moving and aggressively feed after a mid-summer cold snap.

Just as final revisions were being made and this book was heading to press I had another opportunity to test the lateral movement theory. This time, an early cold front grabbed hold and wouldn't let go in late July forcing water temperatures to drop quickly to 74 from 80 degrees, then continuing down to 70 degrees throwing the post-spawn channel and summer cats into an all-out shut down. While fishing was getting tough, I put lateral movement into practice and moved off current. It didn't take long to realize that the fish moved shallow out of the main current and were right where they needed to be. We managed to stay on fish putting together a respectable day while others were struggling to catch fish. That's more proof that understanding how water temperature and metabolism dictate how a catfish lives and that lateral movement really puts big cats in the net.

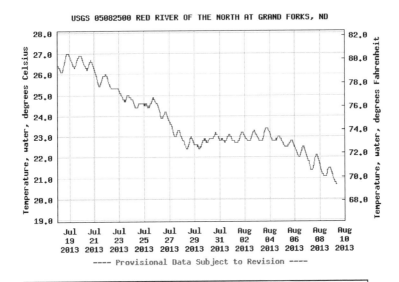

USGS 05082500 RED RIVER OF THE NORTH AT GRAND FORKS, ND

---- Provisional Data Subject to Revision ----

This chart shows the dramatic cool down in July and August of 2013. This presented a perfect opportunity to put lateral movement into play just as this book headed to press.

LATE SUMMER INTO FALL

The terms late summer and fall can be misleading depending where you live as you read this book. The reason for mentioning late summer at all is because in the northern states, late summer begins with cool nights that may spur the fall bite sooner than the traditional fall time that is experienced in warmer southern states. Late summer and fall in the North Country tends to be late August into early October.

During the summer pattern, there always seems to be one cold front that hits and holds on for two to three days causing the water temp to drastically fall. It can drop anywhere from three to seven degrees in a matter of a couple days and shut fishing down. As mentioned in the summer pattern section, the main weather indicator to observe is the sharp barometer drop that is followed by cool to cold and usually windy days.

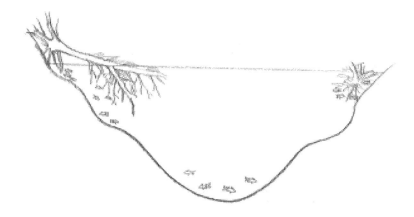

The graphic above shows lateral movement situations. When the fish are feeding aggressively they will be at the bottom of the channel running in the main currents. When the metabolism falls or there are negative conditions, the catfish will move out of the current and into the snags or lay downs near faster water until conditions improve.

Just as a summer cold front will slow the bite, fall is a time when it becomes more critical to move laterally shallow and fish slower to keep catfish coming into the boat. The sharper the temperature drop, the longer it will take a fish to get past the shock factor and into a feeding mood. Usually a fish needs three to five days to acclimate and return to aggressive feeding. Even then, sometimes (especially when the water is in the 50s and falling), the fish will just pick at the baits rather than slam them. This is the time you must be at the top of your game as far as hook setting goes. Everything begins with paying attention to your rod tip. The traditional "circle hook rod bend" may or may not happen during these times. Sometimes you will only see a slight bend in the rod as the fish tastes the bait. If you don't use circle hooks you may simply detect a pickup but not a pull. This is a critical time to find the point where you can help the fish out by setting a hook.

A great way to combat a fall light bite is to simply lighten up your gear. Go to a lighter action rod and lighter sinkers. This simple gear change can mean a huge difference in the success rate of catching these cooler water catfish.

Water temps in late summer and fall will continue to drop as fall progresses. When the water temperature drops below 50 degrees and into the 40s, a fish's metabolism rate enters into the near lethargic zone. This is the time when the fish only need to eat a small amount (one or two percent of body weight) once per week to survive. It is a time when river channel cats move to the deep wintering holes and begin the long wait in the north. They will bite, but catch rates fall greatly and become somewhat unpredictable just as they are in the spring after ice out. The only difference is they feed less. In areas where the water temperatures can stay in the 40s or above in the winter, the channel catfish bite will remain as they are in the fall bite for the most part. Watching temperature patterns and fishing aggressively on a temperature rise and slower on a temperature fall you can have channel catfish success all winter long.

While this late summer and fall pattern can be a nightmare to some northern anglers, myself included, I needed some terrible days on the water to discover the metabolism theory. For years there were more poor to mediocre days than great days.

October 2010 we were coming off a fall flood that shut the guide service down in mid-September. The fishing before the flood was outstanding and of course there was no fishing for three weeks while flood conditions lingered along the Red River.

When the ramps re-opened and people started to make their way out for a last hurrah for catfish the word on the street was bleak. Then the weather turned and we were experiencing high 70s and 80s for the daytime highs. (In Mid-October North Dakota this is rare.) I ran into a gentleman who had been out fishing and he was telling me how great the fishing was that day.

I could not take the suspense so I went out to see for myself the next day. It took some searching and when I found the catfish on the aggressive feed at that point in October I was dumbfounded. It was a magical week that ended abruptly with a sharp cool off. When I began the research for this book I had to take a look at that week to see why it was so great then so bad. What I found was the water temperature had been stable. Then, with the warmup, the metabolism rose and the fish went into a strong feed.

The river was on the high side of the optimum flow range and the water temperature was in the low 50s and rising. Put the two together and we had a catfish bite that would rival any spring pre-spawn bite. The action went on for about a week before a cold front came though bringing with it more seasonal temperatures. In just a couple days the water temperature and the bite had fallen off and back into a normal fall pattern.

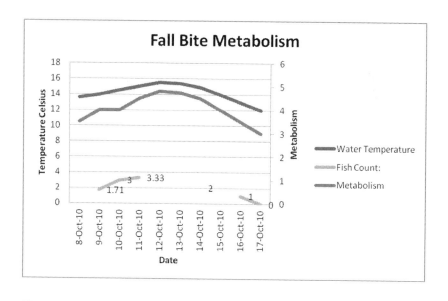

Here's another look at the graph seen earlier in the book. Now it shows the water conditions from the story. The water temperature rises right with the metabolism. Notice the catch rates follow the metabolism as it increases but falls off as the metabolism decreases. (The decrease may have been less had I developed the bite patterns for falling metabolic value in full back then.)

The above photos are a couple of the monster channel cats that turned on during the warm up in October 2010.

LATE FALL AND WINTER

From 40 degrees on down, the channel catfish migrates to the deep holes and starts to hunker down for the winter months. In the northern reaches of the United States the rivers and lakes freeze over. Catching channel cats during this time is a regional act.

In areas where the water does not freeze, the channel catfish will bite all winter long, just more sporadically and lighter than during the other times of year. The fish are usually grouped together in the deepest areas of the rivers or in areas where river lakes open up into slack water with little to no current.

In northern rivers that are ice covered, the catfish tend to go into almost a hibernation period to wait out the winter months. While they will bite, it is very unpredictable as to what the triggers are to feeding. The late Ed "Backwater Eddy" Carlson talked about trying to target channel catfish through the ice on the Red River, near Fargo, North Dakota. He told of the hours he spent watching hundreds of channel catfish in the deepest holes with virtually no movement. Only for a few minutes the fish would feed in an almost frenzy before going back to sitting virtually motionless.

Another indication to the lack of movement in rivers could be proven through hours of video shot by Brian Klawitter showing flathead catfish on the Mississippi River in Minnesota. The fish sat motionless with no desire to feed even when bait is put in front of them. In an interview with Klawitter, he said the flatheads stack up in huge schools and lay motionless with no need to feed.

Klawitter went on to mention that there are catchable channel catfish that position themselves just downstream of the flatheads. He said in his videos he noticed that the channel cats will move up above the flatheads and eventually feed when bait is put in front of them. This is after the bait has spent a considerable amount of time in the area for them to find, inspect, and eventually eat.

Even with those examples of catfish that don't feed in winter, it is evident that catfish move to wide lake areas of river channels and will bite during the cold water months. While they do not require much food to live, they still feed. They are finicky and bite lightly.

Photos Provided by Tyler George

Tyler George from Sheridan, Wyoming, holds ice cats caught in Wyoming reservoirs. George says the key is finding areas holding many catfish and bait. Use lateral movement to stay on the bite.

What this tells us is that catfish move out of the areas of current and into the deep reaches of lakes where they continue to feed just as they do in the late summer and early fall in the shallows. It is almost lateral movement in reverse.

Tyler George from Sheridan, Wyoming, has made winter catfishing on reservoirs look easy. He tells me that the best winter channel catfishing is on the upstream end of reservoirs where there is still some current. He also says the best places for winter catfishing are areas with high concentrations of channel cats as well as high concentrations of baitfish.

According to George, the catfish will bite all day in the deeper portion of the channel. At peak times such as morning and evening and into the night, fish will move laterally out of the main current to more shallow areas to feed. Just as Klawitter said, bait must be left for a considerable amount of time before fish will inspect the bait then feed. This is consistent with all other cold water feeding.

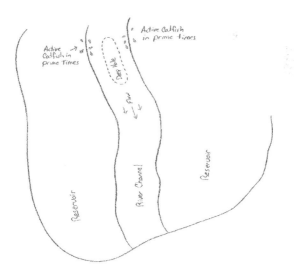

Above you see a drawing of a reservoir with a river channel that runs through it. During the winter months the catfish will tend to congregate at the headwaters of the old river. Fishing near or around the deeper pools works well but the fish will move laterally to the edges of the channel during peak times.

To catch these winter catfish, lighten the gear as much as you can, keep contact with the rod to feel even the lightest bite, and be patient. You can catch channel catfish in certain areas during the winter through the ice.

CHAPTER 12
HOW 21st CENTURY ELECTRONICS HELP CRACK THE CODE

And now finally, we come to using modern fishing electronics.

It is important to understand river behavior and how channel catfish react to its conditions. Understanding the basics of how a channel catfish swims through the seasonal progressions is one thing; understanding the subtleties and details of movement and location will allow you to fish considerably faster -- and hopefully put more trophies in the boat. The ability to understand and recognize where the fish are and might be using modern electronics will increase success.

Many anglers of the past couple decades could not fathom fishing without electronics. Most anglers today still use only a simple graph that tells them water depth, fish location and maybe water temperature. Over the past decade new technology has come into play that has revolutionized angler catching efficiency.

The addition of Global Positioning Systems (GPS) and side imaging takes a fisherman's ability to see and learn what is under water with pinpoint accuracy to an entire new level all together. Side imaging technology allows you to scan the water's horizontal plane while drawing an accurate picture on the screen allowing you to quickly decipher structure and how fish are relating to it. Then you can use GPS to quickly and easily save that location for future reference.

HOW SONAR WORKS

All fish finders operate using Sonar. Developed during World War II, this technology uses sound waves to "view" underwater objects. A sound wave is produced by the fish finder and sent through the water. At the source, the wave is narrow; however as it penetrates deeper, the sound wave spreads forming a cone, or what is commonly called a beam. When the sound wave encounters something within this beam, it bounces back to the fish finder. By measuring the very small amount of time between when the sound wave was send out and when it bounces back your fish finder calculates the distance and reflects it on the screen.

HOW GPS WORKS

The **Global Positioning System** (GPS) consists of a **constellation** of 24 Earth-orbiting satellites. The U.S. military developed and implemented this satellite network as a military navigation system, but soon released its power and potential to consumers.

Each of the 3,000- to 4,000-pound solar-powered satellites circles the globe at about 12,000 miles mph, making two complete rotations every day. The orbits are arranged so that anybody on Earth using a GPS device can detect at least four satellites "visible" in the sky.

A GPS receiver's job is to locate four or more of these satellites, figure out the distance to each, and use this information to deduce its own location. This operation is based on a simple mathematical principle called **trilateration**.

GPS can be a useful tool after you spend some time on the water and find the spots that produce fish in certain situations. One of many great examples I can relate took place during normal flow conditions. I was fishing and soon detected a pattern I'd seen before and consulted the GPS unit for spots to fish. I fished them. The pattern was so exact it duplicated a previous experience two years earlier.

My guests and I were moving from spot to spot catching catfish along the way. After catching fish in four obviously active spots, my client asked what I was looking for on my depth finder to find the fish. He seemed a bit dismayed when he saw the screen was nothing more than my GPS and I was just navigating from recorded locations.

This technique involved spending many hours of work over previous seasons. Now the work and information was coming together with pinpoint accuracy, which sped up the entire process of putting more fish in the boat.

Two spots found and saved on my GPS years earlier ended up
manufacturing a pattern that produced fantastic fishing. These fish
were from two recorded locations and were caught an hour of each
other -- proof that homework and modern electronics can produce
more catfish.

HOW SIDE IMAGING WORKS

Side Imaging or Side Scan can be used to efficiently create an image
of large areas of the river bottom. Side imaging sonar is a tool that
can be used to map the river and the structure under the water on
both sides of the boat giving you an accurate view of where structure
is and the fish that are hiding within it.

Side Imaging uses a sonar device that emits conical or fan-shaped
pulses toward the bottom across a wide angle. The intensity of the
reflections from the bottom of this fan-shaped beam is recorded in a
series of cross-track slices. When stitched together along the
direction of motion, these slices form an image of the bottom within
the swath (coverage width) of the beam and show the structure and
fish within it.

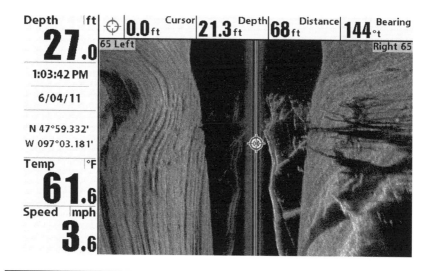

Depth	ft	⊕	0.0 ft	Cursor	21.3 ft	Depth	68 ft	Distance	144 °t	Bearing

Depth ft
27.0
65 Left

1:03:42 PM

6/04/11

N 47°59.332'
W 097°03.181'

Temp °F
61.6

Speed mph
3.6

Right 65

This side image shows a fallen tree under the water. You can see where the branches have merged in the mud and where other branches stick up in the water column. Upon further study you could figure out exactly where catfish would sit in a high water situation. If you look closely at the mid part of the trunk you can see one of the tree's knots. Very accurate side image of a fallen tree, eh?

This is a photo of the tree displayed in the previous side image. It shows the branches that continued into the river bottom as well as the branches sticking up. Notice the knot on the far right.

You now know how the catfish work within their seasonal patterns and how to determine the finer points of catching them based on the river conditions and food requirements. You can fish fast and know what you are looking for from the surface. Now is when you can prove to yourself what you are envisioning and fine tune tactics even more.

If you don't have a high end sonar unit complete with side imaging, that's okay. As you see the movement in the water in the area you believe the catfish are hiding, you can slowly move along the break line on the edge of where you want to fish to try and find the exact point of the drop off or head of the hole with your basic sonar unit. You will see the depth change and be able to mark the spot on a piece of visible structure such as a tree or rock along the bank. Then simply anchor up and cast to the hole, drop off, or eddy.

Just knowing where the bottom drops off into a hole or other piece of structure, or even a tree stump under the water, is a huge step in identifying catfish hiding places. The water surface has already hinted there is something below that may hold fish. Now it is just a matter of having confidence and believing in yourself and taking a shot at presentation.

If you have spent the money on a unit equipped with side imaging, you will be able to stay farther away from your targeted spot and actually draw yourself a mental picture to help see and pinpoint your attack. Having a full image is like having eyes under the water. Besides proving what you already knew from reading the surface you may find other details under water that may hold fish. If you really know how to use a side imaging unit and put extra time into scanning a spot, you truly can find the fish you want to catch -- and actually pick an individual fish to catch! After that all you need to do is catch it.

CATFISH TIP-Don't rely on your electronics for everything. Learn the basics of the fish and the river fundamentals - then utilize the electronics to prove to yourself what you are seeing on the water.

It is kind of funny that as I was growing up and cutting my teeth learning how to catch cats, I used a fairly basic depth finder to find depth and temperature. I would find fishing spots by locating a drop off and drive over it many times until I virtually had a picture of the spot in my head. Sometimes when the catfish were hanging out in the mid-river holes I could drive over it and mark a catfish in the hole. Sometimes I could catch the fish and other times I could not.

When I made a boat upgrade for guiding I went all out and bought the best electronics unit on the market complete with Side Imaging. It took me the better part of a year to learn to effectively understand what I was seeing completely, but I could easily see the drop offs, holes, and underwater structure. That first year I learned a ton about where catfish hang out and even more about my home stretch of river.

There was one thing certain about using Side Imaging: While effective, it is a slow way to fish. Guiding customers pay good money for a certain amount of time to catch fish. Using side imaging while customers are aboard is just too slow a method to find catfish.

As I was learning to read water and recognize channel catfish holding spots on the fly, it became evident that truly understanding catfish and how they operate allows for quick fishing. Once I find the spot the fish should be in or a spot that looks good in a current pattern, I can quickly turn on the imager and take a look and confirm my deduction. Or leave.

Utilizing all that electronics has to offer can be productive, especially on trophy fish. I was shooting with Don Sweet from "Catfishing America" a few years back. The weather had turned on us sending the fish into a negative mood. We had most of our footage already shot, so Don told me we would play a game. I would use Side Imaging to find a fish in an obscure spot that I did not know. We would then mark the fish on the GPS and fine-tune our boat placement to put bait right on the fish's nose.

It took some time to find the right fish but we found him, saved a snapshot of the side image, then used the cursor to mark the bait placement. We turned back re-imaging the areas once again to get a look at the fish. We then set up, cast out, and waited. It took two bait changes and just like clockwork the rock slammed down and a 26-pound post-spawn channel catfish was caught on line and film -- proof that modern electronics are an effective way of picking out your fish and catching it.

Don Sweet, host of Catfishing America, with the 26-pound beast he caught with the help of 21st century electronics including sonar, side imaging, and GPS.

Of course, while using these tools I've learned how to marks spots on the GPS for future reference. This allows me to put together a plan that allows really fast fishing. In fact, sometimes with the fish holding to a solid pattern, it becomes possible for me to fish by simply watching the current seams and only using the GPS unit to get into the precise fishing spot. The technique -- when it works, which is most of the time -- can increase catch rates by as much as 30 percent.

CHAPTER 13
CATFISH CONSERVATION

In Chapter 2, I touched on the topic of the new generation of trophy catfish anglers and how members of this group target trophy fish for the challenge and the sport. Through education and experience, they are good at what they do. This means that the conservation of trophy catfish is more important than ever.

Catfish anglers must be sure to return their trophy fish back into the rivers where they will continue to live and breed stock for the next generations of anglers. Some states have already taken catfish conservation seriously, while other states are not so willing to pursue preemptive measures to protect trophy catfish.

Many states still allow for commercial harvest of channel catfish. Larger fish are taken from the wild rivers and sold to privately owned lakes where the general public pays a fee to catch these trophies in an enclosed environment. Many anglers would see this as no different than hunting deer in a fenced-in area. So much for the concept of fair chase.

Sportsman and trophy hunters are in an uphill battle in these states because the commercial industry continues to grow as angler numbers also grow. This is a lose-lose situation that needs to be addressed by both sides and the state natural resource agencies to find common ground on these practices.

Until that happens it will remain important for all anglers to practice good Catch-Photo-Release on the trophy fish and do their best to keep the rivers healthy with exciting catfish opportunities.

CATFISH TIP-Holding a trophy catfish vertically can cause internal damage to the fish causing eventual death. To take care of your trophy catch always support the fish's weight and hold it horizontally.

FINAL THOUGHTS

Channel catfish in rivers can be caught all year long. The seasonal patterns are an accurate guide to catching fish through spring, summer, fall, and winter. You can catch trophy catfish by understanding how rivers flow, water temperature, catfish metabolism, and other factors as they play into the intricacies of a channel cat's behavior.

By establishing the knowledge base needed for your specific river and learning precisely how each of the factors and patterns relate to it will make you a better channel catfish angler. Most of us fish whenever we can and we go whenever time allows and make the most of it. Hopefully this book will help you make the most of the time you have to chase channel cats.

Just remember, like anything in this world, he who knows the most and works the hardest, wins.

GLOSSARY

River level: River depth is based on how deep the water is at a given gauge. It may also be reported in elevation over sea level. (Also referred to as gauge height.)

River flow: The amount of water transferred through the channel at any given time. It is measured in cubic feet per second.

Water Temperature: The actual temperature of the water as measured by the data collection site. It may be reported in Celsius or Fahrenheit.

Barometric pressure: The force per unit area exerted against a surface by the weight of air above that surface in the Earth's atmosphere.

Moon phase: The appearance of the illuminated portion of the Moon as seen by an observer. The lunar phases vary cyclically as the Moon orbits the Earth, according to the changing relative positions of the Earth, Moon, and Sun.

Catch Rate: Measured in fish per hour (number of fish caught divided by hours fished).

Metabolism: The set of chemical reactions that happen in the cells of living organisms to sustain life. These processes allow organisms to grow and reproduce, maintain their structures, and respond to their environment. The word metabolism can also refer to all chemical reactions that occur in living organisms, including digestion and the transport of substances into and between different cells.

Lateral Movement: Moving perpendicular from the middle to the outside edge of the river rather than parallel up and down stream.

Sit Time: The amount of time given to fish a particular spot.

BIBLIOGRAPHY

1. Stange, Quinn, Smith. (1989). *Catfish Fever*. Baxter, MN: In-Fisherman.

2. Bussolini and Byrum. (2011). *The Catfish Hunters*. Bloomington, IN: AuthorHouse.

3. Canadian Journal of Fisheries and Aquatic Sciences. (2011, April). *Measuring the Bioenergetic Cost of Fish Activity in Situ Using a Globally Dispersed Radiotracer* Canadian Journal of Fisheries and Aquatic Sciences, 1996, 53(4): 734-745, 10.1139/f95-046

4. Jamison L. Wendel and Steven W. Kelsch (1999). *Summer Range and Movement of Channel Catfish in the Red River of the North*. University of North Dakota, Grand Forks, ND.

5. Thomas Wyatt, Aaron Barkoh, Juan Martinez, and Reese Sparrow (2006) *Guidelines For The Culture of Blue and Channel Catfish*. Texas Park and Wildlife Department, Austin, TX.

6. "USGS Current Conditions for North Dakota_ Streamflow." *USGS Current Conditions for North Dakota_ Streamflow*. US Geological Survey, n.d. Web.

7. "Weather Forecast & Reports - Long Range & Local | Wunderground | Weather Underground." *Weather Forecast & Reports - Long Range & Local | Wunderground | Weather Underground*. N.p., n.d. Web.

Captain Brad Durick is a United States Coast Guard licensed catfish guide located on the Red River of the North in Grand Forks, North Dakota. He has spent many years studying channel catfish to learn more about how they adjust to changing conditions that Mother Nature throws at them. Durick has been featured in many media outlets for his channel catfish prowess. He has appeared in In-Fisherman Magazine and Television, Game and Fish Magazine, Outdoor Life Magazine, G3 Sportsman Television, Catfishing America Television, and many other local, regional, and national media outlets.

Brad Durick Outdoors LLC
1640 King Cove
Grand Forks, ND 58201

701-739-5808
braddurick@gmail.com
http://www.redrivercatfish.com

21736240R00088

Made in the USA
Charleston, SC
30 August 2013